D1179007

Pathway of Peace

Pathway of Peace

Pools of Reflection

RACHEL HICKSON

MONARCH
BOOKS

OXFORD, UK, & GRAND RAPIDS, MICHIGAN

First published in the UK in 2010 by Monarch Books
(a publishing imprint of Lion Hudson plc),
Wilkinson House, Jordan Hill Road, Oxford OX2 8DR.
Tel: +44 (0)1865 302750 Fax: +44 (0)1865 302757
Email: monarch@lionhudson.com
www.lionhudson.com

ISBN: 978 1 85424 969 2

Distributed by:
UK: Marston Book Services Ltd, PO Box 269, Abingdon, Oxon OX14 4YN;
USA: Kregel Publications, PO Box 2607, Grand Rapids, Michigan 49501

Photographs courtesy of: p. 28 Chris Atkinson; p. 63 Christine Chouler; pp. 7, 13, 15, 16, 22, 35, 49, 50, 57, 59, 71, 77, 78-79, 83, 93, 94, 95, 99, 103, 113, 114-115, 119, 121, 136 Roger Chouler; p. 40 Simon Cox; pp. 32, 42, 75, 133, 143, 153 Andrew King; pp. 8, 9, 10, 19, 24-25, 30, 37, 55, 65, 67, 68, 86, 111, 130, 132, 134-135, 138-139, 140, 147, 155, 156, 158-159, 160 Gordon Hickson; pp. 26, 39, 61, 89, 91, 117, 125, 127 Estelle Lobban; pp. 104-5 Nick Rous; p. 46 Suzanne Tietjen; pp. 20, 44, 53, 80, 109, 149 Nigel Ward

British Library Cataloguing Data
A catalogue record for this book is available from the British Library.

Printed and bound in China.

Dedication

I dedicate this book to Leila Sienna Paige Douglass, my first grandchild, who has reminded me of the beauty of abandoned trust, rest and sleep, even as a baby! You are amazing, so adorable and I love watching you sleep and rest. May you know the deep love of Jesus in your life always as you discover how to walk on your "Pathway of Peace".

ACKNOWLEDGMENTS

Thank you to each of my friends who have recognized my need and enabled me to find a quiet space to recharge again. Thank you for your care that ensures I do not get exhausted and burned out but remain fresh and passionate as I minister.

Thank you Gordon, my precious husband, for filling the gap in our home and giving me time to reflect, dream and write.

There are so many people who have influenced my life and encouraged me to write and share my story. Thank you to each one of you who has shared your testimony, encouraged me when I speak or shared your life with me. This book has been written because of you.

I also want to thank Tony Collins, of Lion Hudson, for his easy manner and encouraging attitude as we have discussed how to publish this book. It has been a joy to work with you – thank you!

Lastly I owe a debt of thanks to Helen Azer and others who have read, commented on and corrected the script. They have helped me write, examined my spelling, corrected my grammar and enabled me to sound intelligent. Thank you for all your reading time!

Finally, thank *you* for buying this book.

I hope it will be a tool to help fulfil your desire to take time to hear God and relax in His presence. So find a good cup of coffee, get comfortable and begin your journey on this PATHWAY OF PEACE!

Introduction

He will... shine on those living in darkness and in the shadow of death, to guide our feet into the path of peace.

LUKE 1:79

This set of reflections has been written to help you focus on the priorities of your life as you take time to be with God. During these days allow God to touch your heart and position your feet on this path of peace. You need to make a decision that you will make time to eat the word of God and let it focus your life and your future. Maybe you have begun to feel overwhelmed by the pressures of life and you just need to stop, slow down and hear God. Perhaps life has just become frantic, and so busy, that you feel you are only just surviving and you are fearful that you will soon fall

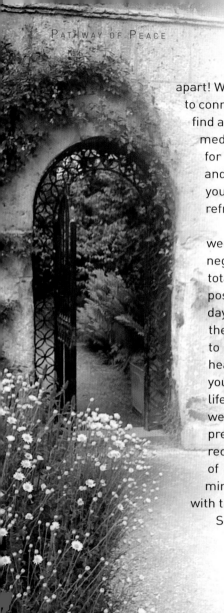

apart! Whatever the issue, you have a desire to connect with God again in a real way and find a new rhythm for your life. This set of meditations has been written especially for you and people who feel pressured and weary. These notes will encourage you to find that time to be still and refreshed in the presence of God.

Experts tell us that it takes three weeks of concerted effort to change a negative pattern of behaviour, and a total of six weeks to establish a new positive alternative. So, this will be forty days (six weeks) of "medicine" from the word of God specifically designed to help you re-establish a more healthy rhythm of life and challenge your areas of stress. For many of us life has become so demanding that we forget how to become still in the presence of God and just listen and receive. As you spend time in the word of God, I believe you can renew your mind and bring your life into alignment with the peace of God.

So let us pray:

"Father, I believe that as I take time to be apart with you, you will reward me with your presence and peace. Teach me to listen and be still and not be anxious!

Father, I trust you to meet with me. I thank you that you are a talking God and you will meet with me as I take time to connect with you. Let me know you more deeply over these days as I start a new journey of discovery.

Thank you, Father, for the Pathway of Peace for my life – today I set my feet on this path and expect to find you!

Thank you, Father! Amen."

So what is the next step? These meditations have been written as a forty-day series, with a new focus for your meditation each week. Each of these topics is a pool of reflection along your journey of peace, where God will touch and communicate with you about your life.

The six topics are as follows:

Week 1 – Absorb His Peace
Week 2 – Awakened by His Voice
Week 3 – Avoid All Distractions
Week 4 – Activate New Thinking
Week 5 – Anchored in His Love
Week 6 – Advance with New Strength

Each day we will read a portion of Scripture, meditate on

a thought for reflection and then focus and pray a prayer of confession. You should try to find a place where you can be alone and relax as you do this. If possible deal with any situation that could interrupt you first, turn your phone off and give yourself a moment of time without pressures! Later in the week find time to read all the words for the complete topic at one time and let the revelation of the week saturate your spirit.

I believe that as you do this, you will watch the word of God begin to refresh your inner being and rejuvenate your capacity. The word will help you recover and take back what the enemy has stolen through your stress and anxiety. It will enable you to think clearly and you will walk out of this season feeling that your life has been revived!

So let us begin to walk on His path of peace for our lives...

Rachel Hickson

WEEK 1
ABSORB HIS PEACE

DAY 1

Peace I leave with you; my peace I give you. *I do not give to you as the world gives. Do not let your hearts be troubled and do not be afraid.*

JOHN 14:27

Thought for Reflection

"Just give me some peace! I need a quiet moment to think! Leave me alone, please!" This cry is heard in homes and offices across the nation daily. But this craving for real peace is only satisfied by finding a resting place internally. In fact, you can experience this true peace even in the midst of external chaos! Our need for peace is essential, and living without it is one of life's curses, and is enough to drive you mad. We read in our Bibles that to wander restlessly throughout the earth, without peace, is one of the torments that the godless and demons experience.

But Jesus stands and gives you peace. This is a supernatural peace. It means that even as a mother, surrounded by screaming toddlers, you can still be at peace. Or, as a businessman travelling on a rush hour train you can find your still place and hear His voice. The peace God gives is not just a quiet feeling: those who have

received it develop a calm and tranquil spirit that is not easily perturbed. It means that when you are going through difficult circumstances you are able to keep a faith-filled perspective and not be overcome with fear. Many people are not able to sleep at night. They are tormented by bad dreams and repetitive nightmares that keep them awake so that they are unable to rest. But God wants to deal with the fear of the darkness and He promises you sleep!

I will lie down and sleep in peace, for you alone, O Lord, make me dwell in safety.

PSALMS 4:8

A heart at peace gives life to the body, but envy rots the bones.

PROVERBS 14:30

Many live in fear of cancer and death, while others suffer from stress-related diseases. These are all symptoms of our lack of peace. So today, take a moment and consciously ask Jesus to give you peace in the inner sanctuary of your life. Study this incredible promise – Jesus gives you His peace, so receive it! Take hold of this supernatural peace and let it overcome your fears.

FOCUS FOR CONFESSION

Thank you, Father, for this gift of supernatural peace. I am so grateful it is a gift that I can receive from you. Teach me to put away my anxiety and learn to receive it without striving. I ask you to touch my life with this deep, true peace. I surrender to you every area where I have become troubled about my health, finances and relationships. I receive this peace. Amen.

DAY 2

What I feared has come upon me; what I dreaded has happened to me. I have no peace, no quietness; I have no rest, but only turmoil. JOB 3:25–26

THOUGHT FOR REFLECTION

This peace Jesus offers us has the power to overcome all fear and dread and give us a real quality of life. So many people live their lives under a curse of fear and superstition. Some are overwhelmed by fear of financial ruin and bankruptcy. They are so controlled by this fear that they become workaholics, never relaxing, and so they find they are never able to rest without worry. Others live with phobias of the dark, fearful of being alone in the house. Still others are tormented by images of their husband or wife having an affair, deserting their home, and abandoning their marriage, and so they become obsessive about their spouse's every action. These tormenting fears rule their lives. This verse states, however, that if you spend your time consumed with thoughts of worry and fear, then what you dread and imagine finally becomes your reality. So, we need to ask God to deliver us from all fear and give us His peace and His way of thinking.

In a meeting recently I had a word of knowledge for a lady who was fearful of reaching the age of fifty-seven. As I gave this word a woman stepped forward saying it was her fifty-seventh birthday that week, and she was terrified that she would die. When we asked her why, she responded by saying her father had died of a heart attack just after his fifty-seventh birthday; then her sister had died aged fifty-seven; and now she was sure her turn was coming! We prayed and broke the power of this deceptive lie that ruled her life, and declared that what she HAD feared had no power to come upon her life! Job states here that what we fear has the power to become our reality, so we need to destroy the deception of our fears and take hold of the truth. We need to uproot and expose the power of fear in our life, and receive a deep revelation and knowledge of our relationship with God, and His promise that He will never leave us. Again and again the Bible uses this expression – "Do not fear for I am with you!", so we need to believe this truth and extinguish every fear with this word.

But the Lord said to him, "Peace! Do not be afraid. You are not going to die." So Gideon built an altar to the Lord there and called it The Lord is Peace.

JUDGES 6:23-24

Gideon had exactly this kind of encounter with God. He was terrified he would die if he obeyed what God was asking him to do. But in the midst of his fear, God appeared to him and he had a revelation of God as his "Peace". His fear and insecurity melted as he experienced the presence of God, and the door of intimacy opened where Gideon discovered the "God of Peace"! So today, hear the sound of God speaking into your life, bringing peace and destroying the control of fear. The enemy uses the weapon of intimidation again and again, and we are convinced we are going to die and be utterly humiliated. But God has a different plan for your life. He speaks this over you – "YOU WILL NOT DIE but you will live and declare the goodness of GOD."

FOCUS FOR CONFESSION

Father, I thank you for peace that overcomes every fear. I ask you now to search my heart and expose the hidden fears or anxieties that control my life. Reveal to me the areas of restlessness and lack of peace, and let me close the gateways that allow these thoughts to control my life. I ask you today for a gift of revelation so that I will have a new awareness of your word in my life. Let me encounter the God of peace. Touch my life: body – soul – mind and spirit. Thank you for your gift to me. Amen.

DAY 3

If it is possible, as far as it depends on you, live at peace with everyone.

ROMANS 12:18

THOUGHT FOR REFLECTION

What is your reputation in the neighbourhood where you live? With the TV programmes showing "nasty neighbours" and the councils issuing writs against unruly teenagers, we need people prepared to live at peace with everyone! But is this possible?

Yes, but it is impossible to live and create an atmosphere of peace if there are broken relationships or a lack of forgiveness in our lives. This peaceful lifestyle has to have at its core a deep commitment to generous forgiveness. We are familiar with the expression – "Go in peace" as it is used so many times in the Bible. But this greeting means so much more than just "have a good journey". It literally means "go, knowing that you have our blessing", or "go, with the knowledge that you have a right relationship with us". Many relationships are so fractured, bringing stress and strife into homes. We need to be generous with our forgiveness of others, as only then will we have peace with God. True peace comes from a rightly positioned or righteous relationship, so if there are areas of bitterness it is impossible to have a peaceful heart. We need to forgive even those who betray us and wound us if we want to have peace in our life.

Blessed are the peacemakers, for they will be called sons of God.

MATTHEW 5:9

Peacemakers who sow in peace raise a harvest of righteousness.

JAMES 3:18

A daughter betrayed her father's trust, slept with her boyfriend and was now pregnant. Eventually she decided she must talk to her dad, a pastor in the local church. She shared her story and asked for forgiveness and for help with her growing responsibilities, pleading to be allowed home. However, this father was not able to see past the humiliation of this illegitimate child and rejected his daughter's pleas for forgiveness. Finally, the time of the birth arrived. The mother pleaded with her husband to forgive his child and visit the hospital, but he refused. Eventually this home was torn apart by the conflict; the father lost his relationship with his daughter, grandchild

and wife and ended up alone, depressed and suicidal. He had no peace because he would not forgive!

My husband has an incredible gift of bringing peace into tense and difficult situations. He often pleads with people to let go of their differences and choose reconciliation, frequently using this expression – "It is better to be reconciled than to be right!" By this he means that it is more profitable for your life to let go of legitimate offences and forgive, than to stand on your rights and lose a whole relationship! We need to be peacemakers in the office and homes where we live, bringing the sound of mercy rather than critical judgment; being generous with our forgiveness even when people have wronged us. If we sow peace we will reap amazing harvests that will last a lifetime!

FOCUS FOR CONFESSION

Father, I ask you for the grace of generous forgiveness. Please examine my heart and show me where I have not released forgiveness and so have lost my peace. Make me a person known for my peaceful nature and one who sows peace in my relationships. Let me be a peacemaker in my home, work place and community. Teach me your path of peace. Amen.

DAY 4

You will keep in perfect peace him whose mind is steadfast, because he trusts in you.

ISAIAH 26:3

THOUGHT FOR REFLECTION

In society today, we tend to become cynical and adopt a negative perspective on life as we watch the TV constantly telling us more bad news. The way we think will affect our ability to walk in paths of peace. So what is this *perfect* peace? In the Middle East you often hear the greeting, "Shalom", taken from this Hebrew word for "peace" and it has a broad meaning. It literally means this: to be safe, to be healthy and happy and to have friends. In other words to be healthy, wealthy and safe! It is a greeting wishing the recipient to be wholly well and to be at rest and satisfaction in body, mind, soul and spirit. This is the peace we are releasing!

When I was in my early teenage years my Granddad was dying in hospital and I went with my mother to visit him. I remember my mum asking him if he had found real peace and if he was ready to die. His response was that he was all right as he was, at peace with himself. But my mum pointed out that the real issue was whether

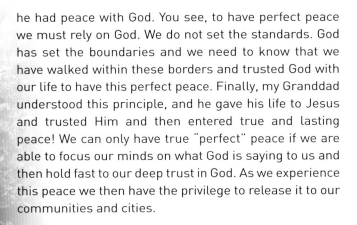

he had peace with God. You see, to have perfect peace we must rely on God. We do not set the standards. God has set the boundaries and we need to know that we have walked within these borders and trusted God with our life to have this perfect peace. Finally, my Granddad understood this principle, and he gave his life to Jesus and trusted Him and then entered true and lasting peace! We can only have true "perfect" peace if we are able to focus our minds on what God is saying to us and then hold fast to our deep trust in God. As we experience this peace we then have the privilege to release it to our communities and cities.

I will grant peace in the land, and you will lie down and no one will make you afraid. I will remove savage beasts from the land, and the sword will not pass through your country.

LEVITICUS 26:6

Also, seek the peace and prosperity of the city to which I have carried you into exile. Pray to the Lord for it, because if it prospers, you too will prosper.

JEREMIAH 29:7

As we partner with God, through us He is able to grant peace to the geography around us and change the atmosphere. We are able to leave a blessing of peace upon a home when we visit people. The Bible shows us that if people give us hospitality and welcome us, we can leave them a blessing of peace. We have the privilege to carry the good news that is the news of peace. The spiritual shoes on our feet are called the "shoes of peace", so that wherever we go we should be ushering in this atmosphere of peace, order and safety. How beautiful on the mountains are the feet of those who bring good news and proclaim peace! Let us put down kingdom footprints of peace on the streets of our broken cities and depressed communities!

FOCUS FOR CONFESSION

Father, let me be a carrier of this peace. Help me to position my life in an attitude of trust so that I may know this perfect peace. As I meet people let me carry an atmosphere of perfect peace into their wounded areas of pain. Teach me to pray for this peace and bring peace to my city and land. Amen.

DAY 5

For he himself is our peace, who has made the two one and has destroyed the barrier, the dividing wall of hostility, by abolishing in his flesh the law with its commandments and regulations. His purpose was to create in himself one new man out of the two, thus making peace, and in this one body to reconcile both of them to God through the cross, by which he put to death their hostility.

EPHESIANS 2:14-16

THOUGHT FOR REFLECTION

In the New Testament the Greek word *eirene* which is translated as "peace" has at the core of its meaning a strong sense of reconciliation. This word was used to express the repairing of fractured bones that were knitted back together and healthy once again: the bone was said to have come to "peace". This peace literally means to bring together fractured parts into a place of relationship and rest. It is the ability to press through the opposing opinions, cultures or doctrines and to be able to put these differences to one side, and to discover the person hidden behind the wall of different beliefs, and then form a real relationship with them based on the true identity of this person or situation.

When Gordon, my husband, first moved to Watford he attended the citywide pastors' gathering and soon discovered that several of the ministers were uncomfortable with his presence as their theological background was different. Gordon then realized that there was one minister in particular who was more negative and very outspoken about Gordon and our church. So Gordon decided he should be a messenger of peace and offered to take this minister out for lunch to a good restaurant, all expenses paid! The minister was so surprised that he quickly accepted. Over this meal these men discovered that they had more in common than they realized. They had been to similar schools, the same university and had several mutual friends. Over the next years they met to pray together regularly one morning a week and finally cooperated in community projects in the town. When the time came to move to the next appointment, these men had become good friends and the wall of hostility had been demolished – in fact, my husband cried as this minister retired and said goodbye! The wall of division had gone!

Too long have I lived among those who hate peace. I am a man of peace; but when I speak, they are for war.

PSALMS 120:6-7

Unfortunately, such circumstances are true of so many of our church situations and family relationships. People are often more concerned with protecting their personal preferences than they are about maintaining good relationships and as a result many innocent people get injured and confused in the fighting. But let us become militant people of peace! I believe that we need to cut this path of peace into our society and pioneer a better way for people to relate. We need to build this highway for the "Prince of Peace".

FOCUS FOR CONFESSION

Father, please teach me the language of peace. Please challenge me when I find I lose my peace and become sidetracked by differences instead of appreciating the person. Help me identify the walls of hostility and separation that cause me to lose my peace in my relationships. Let me be a "man of peace" – one who carries this mandate for my life. Thank you! Amen.

DAY 6

The Lord bless you and keep you; the Lord make His face shine upon you and be gracious to you; the Lord turn his face towards you and give you peace.

NUMBERS 6:24–26

THOUGHT FOR REFLECTION

This precious peace is transferable; it can be given and received! So allow the Lord to bless you with peace. Turn your face to Him and let Him give you peace. Identify those areas in your life that quickly become your gateways of fear and stress and allow Him to shine his presence on your life. As His peace invades our life it will change our countenance and people will notice that our faces shine with Jesus.

Once we know that we carry His peace we can then become distributors of this peace. We can command peace to rule in circumstances. Just like Jesus stood up in the boat in the midst of the storm and spoke to the wind and commanded "PEACE", I believe we can also speak to atmospheres and declare "Peace – Be still!" I remember one example of this while we were living in the Philippines working with Reinhard Bonnke on missions. Every night when we came to go to sleep

there were packs of stray dogs that began to howl and bark just outside where we were sleeping. Night after night this noise continued until we were exhausted. One night as the barking started again, a weary desperation gripped me and I opened the window wide and shouted, "In the name of Jesus – dogs, shut up!" The amazing thing was that these dogs stopped their noise, we fell asleep and from that night onwards the dogs did not howl outside our window again. I was shocked – but so grateful for sleep that it took me a few nights to realize this!

There are also times when panic and fear, which are spiritual atmospheres, can grip our lives and affect our homes. These atmospheres need a spiritual answer – we need to actively release peace. We need to speak to the strife and to these bad atmospheres, whether in the home or at work, and see what happens. He has blessed us with peace so that we can pass on the blessing of peace. I remember when the children used to come in from school tired and irritable, they would often begin squabbling, but if I recognized what was happening I could stop, pray and release the atmosphere of peace and it would give me a peaceful evening.

So let us become instruments of this peace – those who carry the presence of Jesus. We should be the ones who calm the storms of volatile emotions, and stop the arguments and backbiting in the office, because where we go there should be peace and not chaos!

FOCUS FOR CONFESSION

Father, let your peace shine on me... as I lift my face to yours let me know the presence of your peace in my life. Teach me to be a carrier of this peace so that I can influence atmospheres and bring your presence into the places of confusion and darkness. Let me treasure the atmosphere of your peace and keep my life rightly positioned so that I do not lose this sense of your presence on me. Amen.

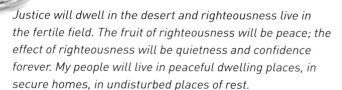

DAY 7

Justice will dwell in the desert and righteousness live in the fertile field. The fruit of righteousness will be peace; the effect of righteousness will be quietness and confidence forever. My people will live in peaceful dwelling places, in secure homes, in undisturbed places of rest.

ISAIAH 32:16–18

Consider the blameless, observe the upright; there is a future for the man of peace.

PSALMS 37:37

THOUGHT FOR REFLECTION

Often when we think about peace, we imagine a quiet lake in the early morning, where the water is as still as glass, the air is cool and the silence penetrating. There is no disturbance, no noise! So we may feel that if we are to be people of peace we need to be very accepting of others and we should not be confrontational. As we live in today's culture we may feel that we should toe the line, be politically correct and not cause conflict. After all, if we are Christians we should keep the peace! But here is the greatest danger! Many of us, by our silence, have begun to say with the false prophets of old – "PEACE, PEACE" – where there is no peace. We have tried to be more sentimental than God. We need to realize that there is a sense in which this is a violent peace! We need to realize that peace ONLY exists within the boundaries of righteousness. So we have to confront wrong attitudes to bring people to peace! If we want to see true peace in people's lives then we have to be willing to confront issues – this peace is not passive - this peace is not soft and fluffy – this peace is not for the weak but the strong.

In these days there is such a cry for peace. People are terrified that they could lose their homes; they no longer feel secure in their jobs, so we must not let the spirit of our culture control our mindsets. We need to rest and think like God thinks! He says to you – *My people will live in peaceful dwelling places, in secure homes, in undisturbed places of rest.* We do not have to live like everyone else – we can live in peaceful places and secure homes. I remember when we returned from Africa to live in the UK in

1990. The housing market was so expensive and we did not know how we would find a place to live in the area of our church. Soon the pressure of our circumstances began to ruin my peace, I felt overwhelmed and Gordon and I began to argue. Our lives lost their grace and our children were anxious. Then one day God spoke to me so clearly – "Be at peace!" I knew I must obey. I began to take time to pray and walk the dog and deal with my fears and anxiety. As soon as I began to cry out for help, God heard my cry, then we were given significant gifts and the perfect house became available: in fact we were able to buy my childhood home as my parents moved to the USA. God had it all in hand, but I needed to learn the secret of living right first, for God always has a future for the person of peace.

FOCUS FOR CONFESSION

So, Father, I commit my life to the path of peace. I want to learn to walk in this attitude whatever my circumstances. I thank you that you love me and you are so good to me. Amen.

WEEK 2

AWAKENED BY HIS VOICE

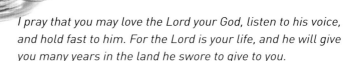

I pray that you may love the Lord your God, listen to his voice, and hold fast to him. For the Lord is your life, and he will give you many years in the land he swore to give to you.

DEUTERONOMY 30:20

THOUGHT FOR REFLECTION

Did you know that God thinks you are amazing and He loves talking to you? This incredible God, who created the universe, then looked for a friend and decided that He would share the secrets of His heart with mankind. What a gift we are given in our communion with God. So God desires fellowship with you. He wants a real life connection of relationship where we choose God and allow Him to speak into the depths of our being and awaken our love. As we listen to His voice of love speaking into our lives it will awaken our desire to know Him. God has a purpose for our lives. Nothing is by accident in the economy of God. Before we were even born, God knew the detail and the depths of our personality. He knew our race, our culture, our intellect and our gender and wove all these facets together with our destiny. None of our complex combinations of call, character and ability shock God. He knows our weaknesses and strengths

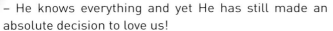

– He knows everything and yet He has still made an absolute decision to love us!

Look again at the Scripture above. Will you love God? Will you, in return, make the choice to love Him, listen to Him and follow his mandate and pattern for your life? Our obedience and yieldedness are our true demonstration of our love for Him. Will we be passionate lovers who are diligent co-workers with His word for our life? For it is only as we align our lives on His path of purpose that we will live life to the full! Before you were born, He set you apart, and He imprinted into the depths of your DNA His calling and purpose. Your spiritual calling was not given to you when you were born again; it was hidden within you when you were physically made. He created your destiny spiritually before you were born, but when you choose to love God you activate this latent destiny. Now you have the opportunity to fulfil this mandate hidden within you.

For each of us there is a path of peace along which we will discover true life! For many years I resisted the calling on my life to be a teacher/preacher among the nations. I did not want to face the controversy of being a woman speaker, so I hid. I volunteered for Sunday School and enjoyed working with the children, I taught in the women's Bible study but I avoided any other invitations. But God began to speak to me and confirm words given to me at my baptism and during my childhood saying that I would go to the nations and speak for Him. He disturbed my excuses and overwhelmed me with His love until I could not resist the sound of His voice asking me to obey. His word becomes like a fire, but if this word is shut up in your bones and you don't action it, you become frustrated! However, if you allow His love to draw you with His kindness into obedience – through every barrier of fear – what joy you experience as you live the life planned for you by God. So today listen to Him, love Him and obey and then you will be satisfied and happy!

FOCUS FOR CONFESSION

Father, I thank you so much that you are a talking God and that you speak to me. I will listen to your voice and I will hold fast to your sound in my life. I believe that I will flourish and live life to the full. Thank you that as I love you, I will hear your voice and that it is easy to hear and recognize your sound of tenderness in my life. I choose today to go your way and to awaken the destiny hidden within my life. Thank you for your word in my heart. Amen.

DAY 9

At this my heart pounds and leaps from its place. Listen!
Listen to the roar of his voice, to the rumbling that comes
from his mouth. He unleashes his lightning beneath the
whole heaven and sends it to the ends of the earth. After that
comes the sound of his roar; he thunders with his majestic
voice. When his voice resounds, he holds nothing back. God's
voice thunders in marvellous ways; he does great things
beyond our understanding.

JOB 37:1-5

THOUGHT FOR REFLECTION

Usually, we are aware of the intimate sound of our
Father's voice speaking tenderly to us. But the voice of
our God is not always quiet and gentle! The Scripture
also refers to the sound of God's voice as thunder or a
loud roar. I remember while we lived in Africa, we had the
privilege of visiting "Masai Mara Game Park" in Kenya.
One evening while out driving in the open-topped safari
truck we heard the sound of a lion roaring. The hair on
the back of my neck stood up as it filled me with a strange
mixture of awe and fear. What a majestic sound, so filled
with power, but also so filled with danger! Once it was
quiet again and the moment of wonder had passed, our

guide turned to us and said, "We call him the KING of the jungle – listen to his roar!"

Often, we have our personal preference for the sound of the voice of God when He speaks to us. We need to realize that the voice of God has many ranges – it can be violent and loud or still, soft and gentle! We need to awaken to the full range of the sound of His majestic voice. Do not limit the style or the ways in which God can speak to you. Let the majesty of His voice fill you with awe for He is the KING of KINGS! Let the voice of God take your breath away! Let the sound of His cry fill you with awe and wonder. He is a marvellous God.

Deep calls to deep in the roar of your waterfalls; all your waves and breakers have swept over me.

PSALMS 42:7

Have you heard His voice like the sound of rushing waters? Another time I was standing in Canada with my husband by the Niagara Falls. We had walked right up to the point where the water cascades over the rocks, plummeting to the depths below. It was difficult to speak over the roar of the water and so we just stood and watched, mesmerized by the water. As I stood still, I felt God speak to me and ask, "Now do you understand how much I love you? I want you to hear the strong sound of my love for you. It is a love so powerful and overwhelming!" That day I heard His voice like the sound of the rushing waters, the roar of the waterfalls. As the mist from the Niagara River wet my face, so my tears flowed and I heard the roar of His voice shouting that He loved me!

FOCUS FOR CONFESSION

Father, I thank you for the many ways that you speak: sometimes it is still and intimate and at other times it is the roar of your majesty. Lord, I thank you that your range of communication with me is so vast. Thank you for your voice. Thank you that you are teaching me this variety as I walk with you on this path of peace! Father, I thank you for your voice like rushing waters. Let this water – the water of your voice – touch my soul. Jesus, touch and refresh me in the innermost parts of my life; your voice is like water to my soul. Father, as your words touch my life let me know the glory of God come upon me. Amen.

DAY 10

The watchman opens the gate for him, and the sheep listen to his voice. He calls his own sheep by name and leads them out. When he has brought out all his own, he goes on ahead of them, and his sheep follow him because they know his voice.

JOHN 10:3-4

THOUGHT FOR REFLECTION

I am utterly convinced that most of us hesitate to obey God because we are insecure, not because we are rebellious! Our problem is this: we are not sure that we have heard the voice of God accurately and so we are fearful of stepping out on a word that may later prove to be false. We need to know that we know the voice of our Father.

Each one of us has the ability to recognize the voice of God. We have a "God receptor" and need to tune our spirit to "hear" the sound of God in our life. It is like tuning your satellite dish to receive the correct wavelength for your television. In the same way we can position our lives to hear God. If we increase our talking time in prayer, God will share His heart with us. Increased prayer will always increase revelation in your

life. Unless we communicate to God, we never give Him the opportunity to communicate to us. We must give God time to speak with us! People of prayer are always people of revelation!

In our busy culture we are not very good at developing a listening ear. We need to find those still places where we can hear His voice. Often, He will speak to you through nature. Walk by a river and hear His voice... walk in the park and hear His voice... sit in a meadow and hear His voice. Let God lead you and teach you the voice of the "Shepherd".

I remember being terrified as a new mother that I would not recognize the cry of my baby. But as I was at

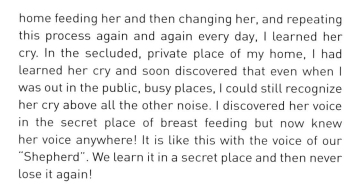
home feeding her and then changing her, and repeating this process again and again every day, I learned her cry. In the secluded, private place of my home, I had learned her cry and soon discovered that even when I was out in the public, busy places, I could still recognize her cry above all the other noise. I discovered her voice in the secret place of breast feeding but now knew her voice anywhere! It is like this with the voice of our "Shepherd". We learn it in a secret place and then never lose it again!

FOCUS FOR CONFESSION

Jesus, I thank you that you know my name and you are calling me in such a personal and special way. I thank you that you are the one who is leading me on my Pathway of Peace and that you go ahead of me EVERY step of the way. I know that you will guide me completely and I do not need to fear. I know your voice and so I can walk and follow on this "Pathway of Peace" in this season. Amen.

DAY 11

O house of David, this is what the LORD says: "Administer justice every morning; rescue from the hand of his oppressor the one who has been robbed, or my wrath will break out and burn like fire because of the evil you have done..."

JEREMIAH 21:12

Thought for Reflection

There are certain situations in which God expects us to act and speak out. God has called us to be a voice for the marginalized and for those whose voice is silenced. In these circumstances, God does not hold back His voice and He does not expect us to remain quiet either. He wants us to learn to hear the cry of His heart concerning the broken and mistreated and to act on their behalf. If we remain passive when He is asking us to act we will encounter His face of anger rather than His hand of kindness. Our God has a strong voice for the broken and the hurting and so we must learn this voice on our journey of discovery. People matter to God, they are His prized possessions and He expects us to treat all human beings with great respect.

*Yet their Redeemer is strong; the Lord Almighty is his name.
He will vigorously defend their cause so that he may bring
rest to their land...*

JEREMIAH 50:34

*He will defend the afflicted among the people and save the
children of the needy; he will crush the oppressor.*

PSALMS 72:4

As we understand this aspect of the voice of God we
discover that we do not have to be afraid of persecution
or difficulty as God is on our case! When we feel that we
are being unjustly treated and no one defends us, our
God uses His voice and He speaks out for us and silences
those who fight against us. When I was in a wheelchair
for nine months, just after my serious road accident,
there were several occasions when I encountered the
real prejudice against disabled people and felt very
vulnerable. People would walk past me and look away
quickly and I would sense their embarrassment; or
they would try to talk to me by shouting using stilted
simple English, as if I was mentally challenged or
deaf. There were other times when I just seemed to be
invisible, and no one would help me even when I was
struggling, but I discovered the God who does help
and defend the afflicted. It was amazing how on each

of these occasions, someone appeared to help me or answer on my behalf. Even when you feel no one sees your pain or understands the prejudice against you, remember God will stand with you and find those to speak out against injustice! It is so important that we train our children to love the broken people. Let us be those who develop compassion around us and become like God who defends the poor, needy and marginalized.

FOCUS FOR CONFESSION

Father, I thank you that you will defend me against all injustice. You will speak out on my behalf. Father, open my ears to hear your voice and let me hear your sound of rage against all injustice, let me hear how you have spoken on my behalf, let me hear the many sounds of your voice over my life. Father, teach me to sound like you and respond like you to defend the marginalized. Amen.

DAY 12

*The Lord spoke to me with his strong hand upon me,
warning me not to follow the way of this people. He said:
"Do not call conspiracy everything that these people call
conspiracy; do not fear what they fear, and do not dread it.
The Lord Almighty is the one you are to regard as holy, he is
the one you are to fear, he is the one you are to dread..."*

ISAIAH 8:11–13

THOUGHT FOR REFLECTION

In these days of political correctness it is very difficult to express opinions different to those around us. Often we remain silent when we should speak up and state our position clearly. For we are called to break the sound barrier of all this carefully scripted language that does not honour God and follow His ways. Just as the prophets of old experienced, so now "the strong hand of God" is upon the shoulder of the church and we are being asked to speak what He would say and to overcome our fears.

We have been in a season when we said "peace, peace" when we should have been saying "NO – NO!" But God is challenging us to break our alliance with these ungodly moral choices and asking us to stop wavering and give a distinct sound. We cannot continue to walk in an artificial unity with those that God opposes – we need to make a choice.

This does not mean that our language has to become harsh and critical, but we do have to learn the art of confrontation with true love as the overriding atmosphere. We have to find the language that shows people we utterly love them as individuals as they are, but we love them enough to help them change too! I remember this dilemma as a young parent. You watch your child and feel overwhelming love but you watch their behaviour and know that it has to change! So you have to confront and begin to say "NO"! This often causes your little darling to become a monster, as his preferred mode of action has just been challenged, but with lots of work, correction and hugs they learn the right way and your love grows even deeper.

At this time I believe God is speaking to us, He is challenging us about compromise and asking us to make a distinct sound, but He promises to walk with us and keep us safe. So break the sound barrier of intimidation and speak out – God is listening!

FOCUS FOR CONFESSION

So, Father, I thank you that your strong hand is upon my life so that I will not go in the wrong direction or listen

to the wrong sound. Please protect me from all wrong conflict and conspiracy, and lead me on the safe path. Please protect me from all fear. Please keep me focused on your character and teach me the fear of the Lord. Father, I want your opinion to be the main influence in my life. Let me speak as an echo of your principles and choices. Teach me your way on this journey. Amen.

DAY 13

"Do not be afraid, O man highly esteemed," he said. "Peace! Be strong now; be strong." When he spoke to me, I was strengthened *and said, "Speak, my lord, since you have given me strength."*

DANIEL 10:19

THOUGHT FOR REFLECTION

It is too easy to get overwhelmed and feel disheartened and it is amazing how quickly it can happen. One day life is good and you have a bounce in your step, and then you have a stressful phone call with a friend or a bad day at work where your confidence is challenged and suddenly you are struggling. Criticism and fear are like cancers that drain away our life. We need to militantly guard our heart and mind and protect them from these invasions! So learn to recognize your entry points and vulnerable circumstances. Here Daniel was a young man in a foreign nation, standing alone in his faith, carrying a deep heartfelt cry of intercession for his people. He was feeling overwhelmed by both his spiritual responsibility and physical circumstances when God appeared and spoke to him. At first this God encounter terrified Daniel even further, but as he listened he realized that God's

words were releasing power right through his body: suddenly, he could cope where before he was feeling exhausted and overcome. God speaks into Daniel's being after a time of intense battle, and challenges the fear and anxiety that have begun to grip his life. God releases a word with the opposite "atmospheres" to those that have engulfed him, and he feels their impact give him life. Just as suddenly as he felt overpowered by fear, lack of self-esteem, anxiety and weakness, now, in a moment, as the right words touch his spirit, he gains strength! It is the same for us, too – a moment surrounded by the right sounds and words can pump life back into us when we feel exhausted and ready to give up! So, fight to maintain your peace. Kill all negativity with these powerful words of life.

The Sovereign Lord has given me an instructed tongue, to know the word that sustains the weary. He wakens me morning by morning, wakens my ear to listen like one being taught.

ISAIAH 50:4

As we become convinced of the power of God's words and watch their effect in our life, we can then become those that carry life-giving words for others too. Take a moment to think about people you know who need a word of life. Take some time to stop, reflect and listen for them today. God will give you a message of peace and then you can be part of His hand of hope to someone who is weary. So learn to awaken to His voice, carry His words of life and lift up the broken.

FOCUS FOR CONFESSION

Father, I thank you that as I soak in your word every power of fear and weariness is broken. I resist every torment in my mind concerning my poor self-esteem and my fear of isolation. It is impossible for me to be alone as God does speak to me and He knows my life. I thank you that right now I receive peace and strength after a season of battle. Just like Daniel I know you strengthen me after a time of spiritual warfare and you pour into me words to give me life. As I sit and reflect and listen to your voice I have new strength again! Amen.

DAY 14

I have hidden your word in my heart that I might not sin against you. I delight in your decrees; I will not neglect your word. My soul is weary with sorrow; strengthen me according to your word. Turn my eyes away from worthless things; preserve my life according to your word. Then I will answer the one who taunts me, for I trust in your word.

PSALMS 119:11, 16, 28, 37, 42

THOUGHT FOR REFLECTION

Giving God's word a central place in your life is like having an aggressive antiseptic in your house. It kills any infection before it can start to grow! So take the words of God and let them become the backbone of your thinking and reactions – it is a perfect repellent for sin. You will find that as you give His word the right place, your life will also find its right position. So make a decision that reading, listening and studying time is time you cannot afford to miss.

Remember to cultivate this habit of listening for His voice. When you feel overwhelmed and negative thoughts begin to dominate your thinking or when you feel exhausted and your mind begins to wander, remember to take these thoughts captive and rehearse

His promises and walk out strong!

This is your season for peace and a growing confidence, with your sense of self-worth regained, and now the next stage of discovery is to rebuild your ability to rest in this new found identity. Whereas silence was often the place which reminded you of your loneliness and the isolation of your journey through pain, this series of meditations aims to cultivate an inner solidity where you will be marked by the beauty of God's peace. From this place there will be a reawakening of dreams and a readiness to run the race of life again, trusting in the voice of the "Good Shepherd". So silence all the taunting of the enemy that says you will never change. This is a new season – you will find new peace and strength. You will find that God is more than trustworthy! So sit a while – rest, be thankful and enjoy the creativity of God, and so be healed!

FOCUS FOR CONFESSION

Lord, I know I need to keep hiding your word in my heart. I know that if your word is not a regular part of my world then I tend to stray back into my old thought patterns and I sin. So keep me hungry for your word. Increase in me such a desire for your word. Train my hands to use your word as an instrument of battle. I do not want to neglect my times of being in the word; keep me hungry! Thank you for this journey of peace and restoration. Amen.

WEEK 3

AVOID ALL DISTRACTIONS

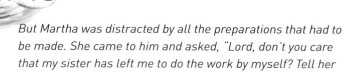

DAY 15

But Martha was distracted by all the preparations that had to be made. She came to him and asked, "Lord, don't you care that my sister has left me to do the work by myself? Tell her to help me!"

LUKE 10:40

THOUGHT FOR REFLECTION

Good intentions need to be followed by decisive actions! So let us make a definite choice to find time alone and seek God. Praying time is never convenient time but always necessary. We must actively carve time out of our busy schedules. So we should take time to relax, listen and wait for God to speak, and deeply desire this intimacy, but it is amazing how even when we make the time our mind will not let our spirit rest. Our lives are so demanding these days and most of us are balancing a hundred different tasks at any one time. So when we do finally sit down we find our minds keep racing with all the jobs we need to remember. Martha was the hospitality queen! She liked things to be perfect for her guests, so she was thinking about the meals that needed to be prepared and what she should cook. Even though Jesus was with her in the house she could not relax and

listen. Martha was aware that she was not coping with all the pressure and she needed help. But, interestingly, rather than ask Jesus to help her focus and get rid of all the distractions, she asked Him to tell Mary to leave the "intimate place" and help her in the "busy place"!

So often we can be the same! We get irritated by people who take time in their schedule to ensure they connect with Jesus. We have even heard the comment "they are SO heavenly minded that they are of no earthly good!" implying that they are always praying and never taking their responsibilities seriously! We can all relate to the cry of Martha – "Don't you care that I am alone and doing all the work!" But Jesus is calling us to alter our priorities, first give Him time in the secret place and then He will empower us in the public place. So do not let the pressure of all your jobs distract you from the place of seeking Him.

Today, make an active decision to make the MAIN thing, the MAIN thing in your life. As you give this time to God He will multiply your productivity. You will be more effective and have a greater focus. Do not let the pressure of the everyday demands of life rob and distract you from the secret place. Make a choice today to focus on having time to listen, reflect and be filled and then go out and live life, knowing that you have increased capacity and strength as you have been in the secret place with Him.

FOCUS FOR CONFESSION

Father, I want to learn to sit, relax and spend time with you without feeling distracted or guilty. Please give me the grace to fulfil my responsibilities. Whether it is what I do in the home or in my office, as I give you time, increase my capacity and help me work quickly and efficiently. Father, let me learn and practise being in the presence of Jesus. Help me focus my thinking and not be distracted with constant busyness as I spend time with you. Keep me from all resentment as I watch other people who seem to have less work and more time with you. Teach me to love this secret place. Amen.

DAY 16

God is not unjust; he will not forget your work and the love you have shown him as you have helped his people and continue to help them. We want each of you to show this same diligence to the very end, in order to make your hope sure. We do not want you to become lazy, but to imitate those who through faith and patience inherit what has been promised.

HEBREWS 6:10–12

THOUGHT FOR REFLECTION

"Nobody appreciates all that I do for them in this house, I feel like I run a hotel not a home!" "I give so much in my friendships, and people just take me for granted and then betray me." "My boss always takes credit for my work." These cries against injustice can become a huge distraction and disturb our times of rest. We serve and work hard but can then feel manipulated and used, and then, once we stop, our mind is full of the turmoil of all our mixed emotions due to the injustice. So, we need to learn to serve people, but see the face of Jesus even in our activity, so that once we stop we can relax and receive our affirmation from God. We need to really hear this promise deep in our being, that our God is

not unjust, and He does not overlook all our work! God watches and sees all our actions, and also knows the attitudes and sacrifices that we make to get the job done. He understands the challenge of injustice when you volunteer to cover a work shift for a colleague and have to cancel a special coffee time with a friend to make this happen, only to find a few weeks later the same colleague refuses to help you when your child is sick!

Years ago, when we were working with a mission organization in Africa, my husband was responsible for finding the housing accommodation for some families. I had just given birth to my second child and I was not well and homeless, too. We were living in one room in a guest house with two children under the age of three, little food and no bathroom facilities. While Gordon was working hard to find homes for the other families I was left alone in this dark, small room. Finally, he found suitable accommodation, signed the contracts and the families moved in. But one family objected. They were unhappy with their home and accused Gordon of doing a poor job. Gordon was not worried, sorted the problem for them and found a different place. But I was left with the issues. I was offended that they were so unappreciative of our work and sacrifice. In time, I found I lost my joy and closeness with God. Every time I prayed I could only hear the sound of my anger and sense of injustice. I was distracted spiritually and my life lost its sense of joy and peace. Finally, after about six months, God showed me that the root of my disturbed spirit was this housing issue. I had opened the door to offence because I had allowed my sense of injustice to rob my peace. Once I released my sense of injustice, the confusion left and the peace returned and I could worship once again!

So, today, remember – God is NOT unjust. Do not allow those circumstances of injustice to distract you and rob your peace.

FOCUS FOR CONFESSION

Father, I thank you that you have watched everything that I have done for you over the years and nothing has missed your attention. Please do not let me get distracted by the "atmospheres" of ungratefulness. I do not want to become bitter or withholding so I thank you that you are just and you reward me for everything I have done. Father, let me press in and not hold back and obtain everything that you have promised me. Thank you so much that you are just and fair and you do give me exactly what you have promised. Amen.

DAY 17

*Finally, brothers, whatever is true, whatever is noble,
whatever is right, whatever is pure, whatever is lovely,
whatever is admirable – if anything is excellent or
praiseworthy – think about such things.*

PHILIPPIANS 4:8

THOUGHT FOR REFLECTION

It is a real discipline to think the best and not the worst about yourself and your circumstances in everyday life! Our negativity can become a real distraction. When somebody compliments us, we immediately react by wondering what favour they require, rather than accepting their words graciously. At a conference in the USA over ten years ago now, a lady came and sat next to me at the end of one of my sessions. She asked if she could take me shopping and spoil me. Immediately, my suspicious nature made me cautious, and then this verse came to mind, "Think the best Rachel and be blessed." So to my surprise I agreed to go with her to a nearby shopping mall and this precious woman spoilt me! In fact, I still have some of the clothes today and love them!

That night, after this amazing shopping experience, I lay in bed and felt overwhelmed and God spoke to me, "Rachel, learn to trust and think about the best and not the worst." So often my prophetic nature tends to lead me to be critical and over-discerning rather than accepting.

I think we can miss so many special bonuses of God, by rejecting simple words and actions that are genuinely given to bless us. So today, make a decision to receive the words and kind actions around you, and don't allow yourself to be distracted by negativity.

When someone seeks to bless you, focus your attitude on the best. Practise being someone who believes in people again, even when they fail you! Take time to think the best! This also applies to your own life, too. Do not think about yourself negatively either: remember God thinks you are the best.

FOCUS FOR CONFESSION

So, Father, I give you my mind and in this season of reflection I will set my mind to dwell on the best and the excellent. I thank you that my life is safe, I will think and dwell on the true, right and admirable gifts that you have given me. I resist every thought that would depress, oppress or suppress my gift – only what is good will occupy my mind. I thank you that you are with me, my mind will be full of peace and not confused by suspicion! Amen.

DAY 18

*Do not be anxious about anything, but in everything,
by prayer and petition, with thanksgiving, present your
requests to God. And the peace of God, which transcends
all understanding, will guard your hearts and your minds in
Christ Jesus.*

PHILIPPIANS 4:6–7

THOUGHT FOR REFLECTION

"A good Mum will always worry about her kids. After all, it is our instinct!" Later, I found myself processing this conversation that I had overheard. Initially, I agreed with them, as my experience demonstrated that most mothers I knew worry about some aspect of their children's lives. Was Simon taking too long to be potty trained? Was Jessica lying about her friendship with this boy? Will I cope when my child becomes a teenager? These, and many other anxious questions, seemed to fill the conversations of mothers as they talked with each other. As a result, I realized I had adopted an attitude that said that if I really cared for my kids I would worry about them! But I remember when God began to challenge this mindset. I had been away speaking at a ladies' breakfast when a woman challenged me and said, "Don't you worry when you leave your children at home alone that they may get involved in something wrong? If you were a good mother surely you would be at home with them keeping them out of trouble?" As she confronted me, I felt alarmed, but suddenly I realized that even if I was with my kids 100 per cent of the time I had NO power to give them life and keep them safe. As I stood in this meeting hall I suddenly knew that worry had NO power to protect my kids, but prayer did! For so long I had believed an ungodly proverb that went something like this: "To be feminine is to be fragile and fearful!" (especially concerning your children!). But God began to show me how to pray rather than worry about them.

So what are your ungodly beliefs that open a door to fear

and anxiety? Do you worry about money and provision? Anxiety and worry are robbers of life, and the stress and pressure that result from their presence crush our bodies and steal our peace. Today, take some time to analyse the areas where you tend to worry rather than trust. What are your triggers of anxiety?

Money was a big area for me in our early days of marriage. If the bank account was getting low I began to panic and control every penny just in case we got a big bill! But God had to teach me how to live my life leaning on the goodness of God. When I was pregnant with David in Kenya we suddenly received a large medical bill and we couldn't pay it. I panicked. Where would the money come from? As I stood in the kitchen, worried and anxious, I felt the Holy Spirit speak to me, "Do you want me to take this job or not?" At first I did not understand and then He continued, "You keep praying and asking me to help you, but then you take this problem back into your own hands and start worrying. Why do you not trust me to get this job done for you?" At that moment, I had a picture come into my mind where you write out a request list and give it to your Father and then He puts it on His desk with His "jobs to do" box. But every time I worry it is like me going to the desk and removing my list from the box and trying to sort it out myself! But we need to leave our requests in the capable hands of a loving God and stop meddling with our worry and fear! Now to finish the story, I did choose to trust God, and within a week all the money was sent to us from people who were just "prompted" to send us a gift!

FOCUS FOR CONFESSION

So I thank you for your guard of protection over me and thank you that worry and fear are no longer going to be part of my personality. Deliver me from all anxiety and reveal to me my patterns of worry. Father, teach me to pray about my needs and not worry. Guard my mind with a deep sense of trust in you. Father, I place a guard over my life at this time and believe that I will live in an atmosphere of peace. Stir a new lifestyle of prayer in me. Amen.

DAY 19

Am I now trying to win the approval of men, or of God? Or am I trying to please men? If I were still trying to please men, I would not be a servant of Christ.

GALATIANS 1:10

THOUGHT FOR REFLECTION

The intimidation of what people think, or the fear of humiliation and embarrassment, limit every one of us at some stage in our lives. Adolescence is often a painful time. This is a season in our lives when acceptance and reassurance is so important. Our bodies are changing and the need to be liked and noticed feels essential. Suddenly, our self-worth is defined by people's comments rather than who we are. We can find ourselves striving to gain approval, altering our value systems to try to fit in with a peer group and feeling the pain and pressure of rejection. Although this journey often starts in the teenage years, unfortunately, it does not always stop there. If we are not careful, we can develop a lifestyle habit where we are constantly distracted by other people's opinions of us rather than our own convictions. Soon we find that we are living life stressed and nervous, always watching for the reactions of our parents, our boss or our friends. We

make decisions that will comply with the expectations and desires of those around us rather than the call of God within us. We find that we are compromising the essence of who we are for the sake of acceptance and appreciation. Slowly, we find that we have sold our soul to this slave called "approval" and we are now caged in a lifestyle that contains us and controls our true passions. Our life is now externally manipulated by people's demands rather than internally motivated by the Spirit of God. It is time to break free!

When you are making a decision, whose opinions really matter to you? Do you listen to the advice of the people who really pray for you and understand your destiny, or does the sound of unsaved family and reason control you more? Where do you look for approval? I realized as I started to function in public life that I wanted to be liked. People's praise mattered to me but this desire was dangerous! God had to train me. Suddenly, after a couple of years of compliments and rewards I began to hit accusation and opposition. I received letters correcting my teaching, debating my views of women in ministry, aggressively attacking my character and even threatening my family. Suddenly, I was not the popular preacher on the circuit! I wanted to run, hide and feel sorry for myself. Like Elijah, I felt I was the only one, and it was so unfair! But God challenged me – "Get

up – I thought you wanted to be my servant – have you asked *me* what I think about your service yet?" In that moment, I realized I had become totally distracted by the assessment of people, but God had been keeping His

record of my service too. As I spent time in prayer, He began to speak to me and I realized that God credited and merited different things. He had watched my generosity to some people in the church, He had seen my care for my home and family, He loved my passion and devotion – in fact He loved ME! Suddenly, the letters were back in perspective, and I realized I needed to hear what heaven was saying about me. This is what really matters! We were never made to be human "doing" machines, but God made us human BEINGS – so relax and be yourself as God enjoys the real you!

FOCUS FOR CONFESSION

Father, please protect me from the curse of constantly striving to fulfil other people's expectations of my life. Father, teach me the real joy of being me! I really want to enter this new season with a deep confidence that my expression and gifts are acceptable to you. Deliver me from all the distractions of trying to please people – or trying to please systems – and let me have such a joy in knowing that I please you. Thank you that I am free from the slave of approval! Amen.

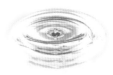

DAY 20

Then he said to them, "Watch out! Be on your guard against all kinds of greed; a man's life does not consist in the abundance of his possessions."

LUKE 12:15

THOUGHT FOR REFLECTION

As I listened to her story I realized how fortunate I was. This dear woman continued, "I remember the first time I had a wardrobe in my bedroom. I grew up in a tiny house and shared my bed with three sisters. We had one set of school and home clothes each and so no need for a wardrobe. But now I was married and for the first time I had money, clothes and space!" This was not a story about a village in Africa, but a town in England just thirty years ago! As I listened to her, I realized how only recently our culture has changed, and now possessions are such a normal part of our expectations of life. We regularly upgrade our gadgets to keep up with the latest trends, we decorate our houses because we get bored of the colour, we buy new clothes when the new fashions arrive in the shops and then we have to spend time getting rid of the abundance of our "stuff"! I do not believe that poverty is near to godliness, but I believe that God

wants us to evaluate our desire for "stuff". At this time, the global economy is struggling and we are watching the results of years of selfish spending and borrowing take effect. The Bible tells us that what we sow is what we will reap. So we need to ensure that the major investments of our lives are into His kingdom not our own lifestyle. There is a huge cultural pressure to grasp and be greedy rather than to live life satisfied!

Today, take a moment to thank God for the possessions that you have. I have developed a simple practice of asking God to extend the working life of my household appliances like my fridge and washing machine, my car and other equipment. Rather than having to change these items so regularly, I ask God to prolong their usefulness so that I can invest in the kingdom more! Let the "atmosphere" of generosity touch you today, and ask God to show you how you can invest more in the kingdom. Resist every attitude of greed and jealousy.

Our culture has begun to define our worth by what we have, but this is such a distraction and deception! We need to be on our guard against these attitudes in our friendships and family, and help each other realize that our life satisfaction does not depend on WHAT we have but on the revelation of WHOSE we are!

FOCUS FOR CONFESSION

I ask you, Father, to protect me from all the jealous and covetous attitudes in our culture. Please give me a new discernment to recognize their power. I commit my home and possessions to you. I trust you to give me the best. I know that I do not need to be greedy and grasping but you will give me the best. So give me a deep trust and revelation of your provision and protect me from every type of greed that could distract me. Thank you. Amen.

DAY 21

But seek first his kingdom and his righteousness, and all these things will be given to you as well. Therefore do not worry about tomorrow, for tomorrow will worry about itself. Each day has enough trouble of its own.

MATTHEW 6:33–34

THOUGHT FOR REFLECTION

This verse is always a challenge to our priorities! In other words, if we take care of God's house and priorities, He promises that He will take care of ours! We cannot just casually hope that we will stumble upon the purpose of God in our lives, but we need to actively seek it. We need to have an intentional attitude of active pursuit, and we need to search for His way with our focused attention! Then, once we know the plan of God, we must align our lives with His desires and then we can watch God take care of all our practical, spiritual and emotional needs.

I believe in these days God is looking for an army of ordinary people who know Him and are not easily distracted by fear, reputation and possessions, but who are ready to be captivated by the face of Jesus. These will be a dangerous generation of Jesus lovers who delight to give their lives away for the kingdom's purpose of

heaven. The attitude of the kingdom is always counter-cultural. We will live our lives in the opposite spirit and attitude to those around us. We should not be fighting to maintain our reputations in the face of criticism but trust God to defend us. We should not be motivated by ruthless ambition to climb the promotion ladder, at any cost, but rather expect God to make a way for us. We should not be consumed with fears about our future as we have a Father who is in control of our destiny and His plans never fail! So, in this season of shaking we may be shaken but we should not be stirred by worry! When financial institutions crumble around us, remember that our lives are NOT built on the sand of man's wisdom but on the rock of God's instruction. Our house will not come down in this storm as we have built on the foundation of Jesus, the "rock of all ages", who never fails.

So, today, do not be distracted by fears for your security and future. Remember, we serve the eternal God and He is in control of our lives as we surrender to, and obey, Him. Fix your eyes on JESUS. He is the starter and completer of this journey of life. Just take one day at a time and enjoy your life. Do not be overwhelmed, but seize the day with your hands of faith and win. You are made to overcome!

FOCUS FOR CONFESSION

So, Father, I fix my eyes on Jesus and on your kingdom's purpose. I have such a desire to honour you. I want to see your righteousness and integrity in my life. I ask you to keep stirring my hunger for you and help me keep focused on your priorities. I thank you that when I ask I will receive, and when I seek I will find; so put a fresh confidence in me to SEEK your purpose. Father, I will take one day at a time, just one day, and not be distracted by the weight of the future – you have my life in your hands. Amen.

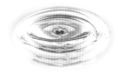

WEEK 4
ACTIVATE NEW THINKING

DAY 22

Do not let this Book of the Law depart from your mouth; meditate on it day and night, so that you may be careful to do everything written in it. Then you will be prosperous and successful.

JOSHUA 1:8

THOUGHT FOR REFLECTION

What an interesting thought! This Scripture challenges us to never let the Word of God depart from our mouths. You would expect it to say – "Don't let it depart from your thoughts". But this instruction emphasizes the principle that if the Word of God is flowing out of our mouths, then it has already soaked into our minds and hearts. For we know that it is out of the overflow of our hearts that our mouths speak! So if the word is on the inside it will leak out through our mouths, and it will just happen automatically! From listening to the way a person speaks we can quickly discover the true passion of their heart. When someone is falling in love, they may deny it when asked, but, as soon as they relax, the name of this person will creep into every conversation and they are not even aware they are doing it! Their heart is given and their mouth keeps letting the secret out!

We also need to meditate on the word day and night. I remember being in a prayer meeting one day and listening to a new believer pray – "God, I thank you that you want me to marinade in your word every day!" We all laughed and corrected her terminology, but today I think "marinade" actually gives us a good picture of meditation! As we read the word, we need to stop and ask God for specific application of this word in our lives. We need to eat the word, like fresh bread, and let the word do its work in our life. Pause, think about the word, and receive fresh understanding and application of the Scripture today. Then, once you know what God is saying – do it! I believe we are living in the "Nike" era, a time in history when God is asking us to respond like the Nike advert and "Just DO it!" As parents, we know the frustration of dealing with delayed obedience. You can ask your children to put their shoes away, and they promise they will do it, but delay as they are watching a favourite TV show. So you ask again, and still there is no response. Delayed obedience IS disobedience! But if we want to reap the full benefits of loving and reading the word, we must become quick to respond.

I remember when we first arrived in Africa to work with "Christ for All Nations", we asked for our instructions and we were told, "Pray, listen, and then just DO what the Holy Spirit tells YOU to do!" So that is what we did, and the miracles were many!

FOCUS FOR CONFESSION

Father, I thank you for the privilege of soaking in your word. Deepen my love for your word. Increase my ability to read it with fresh knowledge and understanding. I thank you that you have created my heart and mind to work together and there is no separation. You have made me able to think and able to feel. Teach me how to be still and listen, meditate on your word and then obey. Give me a new level of satisfaction as I spend time listening and responding. Thank you, Father, that you will teach me to learn your ways. Amen.

DAY 23

*Let me understand the teaching of your precepts; then I will
meditate on your wonders. My soul is weary with sorrow;
strengthen me according to your word.*

PSALMS 119:27–28

THOUGHT FOR REFLECTION

I believe God really wants us to understand the principle
behind His instructions. Once we have a revelation of the
way God thinks and why we have certain principles and
protocols in Scripture, it blows our minds and causes us
to worship!

I remember when I was considering how to talk
to my kids about sex, marriage and virginity. I knew I
could give them the standard
Christian talk of "no sex
before marriage" and ask
them to respect these rules,
but instead I began to pray
and ask God to give me a
specific revelation about
this principle of virginity. As
I prayed, He showed me the
spiritual picture of marriage,

of how Jesus, the perfect "lamb of God", gave His life to His bride. I realized that as He hung on the cross His blood was shed, and then the veil was torn, and so a way was made for us to enter into the intimate place of relationship with God. Suddenly, I saw that

the intimacy of marriage is a flesh to flesh illustration of the greater picture of Christ and His bride. When I shared the full revelation of this image with my kids they understood why sex, marriage and virginity are precious. I then knew it was not just a precept to them, but a precious revelation. If you spend time and ask God to show you, He will teach you and give you understanding. Then you will live your life by revelation and not religious rules, because you will understand and celebrate the incredible ways of God.

Often, we can begin to feel exhausted and spiritually weary, and not know why. Then, we discover that without realizing it, we have begun to live life relying on our own strength. Subtly, our supply has shifted and we are

now desperately trying to resource our lives from our own efforts. Paul puts it like this when writing to the Galatians in chapter 3, verse 3 – "Are you so foolish? After beginning with the Spirit, are you now trying to attain your goal by human effort?" In these seasons, we urgently need a fresh injection of power from the "word" of God. When you have no emotional capacity, take some time and focus on the "word" – it is amazing how quickly you can feel revived! Just as a jug of water can quickly refresh a pot plant that has been out in the heat too long without water, so the "word" of God can reawaken your spirit and make you feel alive again! So don't get weary, but get wet again with the presence of God!

Focus for Confession

Father, I thank you that you can teach us to understand the principles in your word. Let me love your precepts and teach me to live with a real sense of revelation and not just the duty of rules. Show me, Father, when I begin to live my life out of a sense of duty rather than by the power of the Holy Spirit. Refresh me where I have grown weary with your word. Please awaken revelation in my life and let your word renew my spirit again. Amen.

DAY 24

God will speak to this people, to whom he said, "This is the resting place, let the weary rest"; and, "This is the place of repose"– but they would not listen. So then, the word of the Lord to them will become: Do and do, do and do, rule on rule, rule on rule; a little here, a little there...

ISAIAH 28:11–13

THOUGHT FOR REFLECTION

God will always communicate with us, but the tone and language of His voice may alter depending on the receptivity of our heart attitude at the time. Here we read that God wanted to speak to His people and assure them of His compassion for them as they were weary. He wanted them to understand how to enter a place of rest and be restored, but they were stubborn and refused to listen to this sound of God in their lives. So rather than receive the opportunity to be sustained and refreshed, they dismissed God's encouragement and God changed His language, and His voice began to sound just like a set of basic instructions.

This contrast of these two types of dialogue is true in so many of our relationships. When your heart is clear and open, you can pick up the phone and chat in a personal, relaxed style and ask your friend to help you with certain tasks. But if you are irritated, yet still need to talk to this person, your conversation tends to be abrupt, you keep all communication to the bare minimum, and just outline the essential instructions in order to get the job done. We can all recognize this situation in our own friendships. In the same way we can have open, loving conversations with God or just the straight business dialogue. God desires to talk with us as friends, touching our hearts and refreshing our souls, as well as directing our lives. He does not want the straight, austere conversation where He dictates a set of commands to us. He wants heart to heart connection. These conversations take more time, but are so much more rewarding!

Do you not know? Have you not heard? The Lord is the everlasting God, the Creator of the ends of the earth. He will not grow tired or weary, and his understanding no one can fathom. He gives strength to the weary and increases the power of the weak. Even youths grow tired and weary, and young men stumble and fall; but those who hope in the Lord will renew their strength. They will soar on wings like eagles; they will run and not grow weary, they will walk and not be faint.

ISAIAH 40:28–31

So take time to talk. Change your way of thinking when you come into the presence of God. Don't just come and talk to Him in times of crisis, rushing into his presence just to get the next set of emergency instructions to rescue your life. But take time to dream, cogitate, and muse. If you discipline your life to take time to stop and consider God, your life will gain new effectiveness and your intellectual and emotional capacity will increase. Consider God – take some time to soar in the heavens and think about Him. Let your mind wander... let hope revive your expectations and then run! It is time to connect with His incredible plans and be overwhelmed with the God of creation once again!

Focus for Confession

God, I do not want a distant, formal relationship with you, I want to know you! Teach me to connect in real conversations with you. Touch my heart and invade my imagination with your thoughts and perspectives. Strengthen me where I have grown weary and withdrawn. Teach me to ponder and muse about your greatness. Let me see you in greater measure and obey you with greater passion. Amen.

DAY 25

Immediately Jesus knew in his spirit that this was what they were thinking in their hearts, and he said to them, "Why are you thinking these things?"

MARK 2:8

But Jesus knew what they were thinking and said to the man with the shrivelled hand, "Get up and stand in front of everyone." So he got up and stood there.

LUKE 6:8

THOUGHT FOR REFLECTION

I remember a story Bob Mumford told once. He was walking along a beach, talking with God and complaining. God was challenging him to make some changes that seemed unreasonable to Bob. Finally, Bob heard God say – "Bob, you and I are incompatible and I do not change!"

Our reactions and logic often clash with God's way of working. He often offends our sense of reason and even ignores our perception of justice. As a pastor, I often hear this cry of frustration from individuals as they try to grapple with the fairness of God! We love to live by rules and if someone has not prayed as hard, or struggled as long, we feel cheated if they are blessed before us! We can tend to have the attitude – "Wait in line! I got here first – God has to listen to me now!" Here we find that Jesus' actions of compassion towards this man irritate the religious leaders as they wanted to uphold their understanding of correct protocol. Jesus knew what they were thinking; He understood their thought processes and challenged them. Totally aware of the "church politics" of the situation, He ignored their preferred procedure and healed the man, and then asked him to stand up as a public sign. He directly confronted the limited understanding of the religious leaders. He was saying, "I know how you think, but I am not controlled by your traditions and preferred mode of operation – I will touch the poor and needy and heal them!"

So what offends you? Jesus is more interested in revealing the motivation of our hearts than satisfying the logic of our minds. Often, we get caught in offence by our sense of moral justice. For instance, I find it hard when bad things happen to good people, but I find it even tougher when good things happen to bad people! In these situations, Jesus knows what we are thinking, so we need to ask Him to renew our minds and activate a new way of thinking. Do not get offended, but get upgraded, and ask God to help you think like HIM!

FOCUS FOR CONFESSION

God, I thank you that you are good and that your ways will challenge my sense of logic and fairness. Help me recognize the times when what you do is beyond my understanding and keep me from all offence. Father, help me trust even when I cannot process everything, help me know your care even when I feel unable to grasp intellectually all the steps of the journey. Father, teach me to use my mind to love you in a more profound way. Father, activate my mind to think more and more like you. Teach me your spiritual logic and ways. Challenge the areas where I have made rules that have become a hindrance to you working in lives around me. Amen.

DAY 26

Dear friends, this is now my second letter to you. I have written both of them as reminders to stimulate you to wholesome thinking.

2 PETER 3:1

Therefore, holy brothers, who share in the heavenly calling, fix your thoughts on Jesus, the apostle and high priest whom we confess.

HEBREWS 3:1

THOUGHT FOR REFLECTION

Peter, the apostle known for speaking before thinking when he was with Jesus, here encourages us to upgrade our thinking ability. Jesus had to rebuke Peter after he advised Jesus according to natural wisdom rather than godly revelation. In this age of rationalism and scientific logic we need to stimulate our minds to spiritual thinking patterns. Here, Peter shares with us that his passion in writing to the church was to help them stimulate more wholesome thinking.

I am a clinical biochemist by profession. I studied science at university and then worked in medical research. But when I was in the church as a young person, I always felt guilty about loving knowledge and being interested in learning. Somehow, I had developed a wrong belief that my mind was a hindrance to my faith. But now I realize it is not my actual mind or my intellectual ability that are the hindrance to God, but rather my ways of thinking and my teachability that can present issues! We are trained to think in secular and worldly educational systems on the whole and so we need to renew our minds to more wholesome ways of thinking. I believe we need intelligent, outstanding scholars in the church today who are able to use their minds to the full, but who also need to be childlike in their faith. I believe passionately that simple faith and academic ability are a perfect combination. But we need God to help us.

So we need to fix our thoughts on Jesus. Identify those areas where you doubt and struggle to simply believe God. Ask Jesus to give you a spirit of revelation in your mind so that you can believe! Most of the battles of our faith are those we fight between our ears, in our mind! We can battle intellectually with issues like evolution, we can feel challenged by philosophical questions like suffering in the world, but if we keep focused on Jesus we will not get confused.

Ask God today to activate new thought processes of revelation. Access new downloads from heaven and know that He can stimulate your mind. Even when you feel that you cannot think clearly, ask God to strengthen your mental capacity and rest secure – you can have a faith-filled, thinking life!

FOCUS FOR CONFESSION

Father, I ask you to stimulate my intellectual capacity. So often I have been afraid that my mind is a hindrance to really knowing you. But, today, stimulate my mind to access new revelation. Right now I ask you to touch my mind – the conscious, unconscious, dream centre and semi-conscious parts of my mind and breathe on them by the Holy Spirit. Lord, let me use my mind for you. When I feel overwhelmed by problems or intellectual questions teach me to be Jesus-focused and so find my solution. Teach me your way of wholesome thinking! Amen.

DAY 27

For the word of God is living and active. Sharper than any double-edged sword, it penetrates even to dividing soul and spirit, joints and marrow; it judges the thoughts and attitudes of the heart.

HEBREWS 4:12

THOUGHT FOR REFLECTION

As we soak ourselves in the word of God, we discover it exposes deeply hidden traits of behaviour and ways of thinking. Seasons of reflection and lingering in the word of God are so important if we want to grow. We need to let the word do its deep work. Don't start digging to look for your defects and problems. But let God uncover the problem areas using His Word. When the "word" of God is used correctly it is like precision laser surgery. It goes right to the root of the issue, exposes it, cuts it off and removes it with minimal damage, leaving the surrounding areas healthy and full of life. When we position our life in the presence of the Word, we will be convicted, our choices will be challenged, our motivations confronted, but we will start to live with a new freedom. You will find that your responses instinctively start to become godlier as you are being changed to think and react like Him!

It is time to react and respond in this new way that will not make "sense" but is necessary for life. When people treat us badly, our instinct is to react by withholding our friendship, but God's way for us is to still live with an open heart towards them. The way of the Kingdom is always upside down. When we feel betrayed, we are called to trust. When we are persecuted, we are told to bless. When we are poorly treated, we should respond with generosity. We are called to go in the opposite spirit to that which comes against us. This takes practice and requires a renewing of our minds. We need to activate a new way of gracious thinking that is not human but supernatural.

This type of generosity requires discipline and determination. When Gordon and I were going through a tough time of opposition, where our motives were being challenged and our reputation damaged, it was so hard to keep loving, especially as some of the people involved had been very good friends. My heart began to close towards these people and I found myself withdrawing. I desperately did not want to get bitter. I wanted to keep sweet, but I was struggling. So I got up early, and I was praying when God asked me why I had delayed in buying a gift for this friend's birthday. "Father, I can't. I am too hurt, she is speaking against Gordon and I, how can I give her a present?", I complained. But God challenged me – "I do not change nor should you – bless her!" So I did, and although there was no change at the time, when we connected years later she remembered that I had bought her this gift and she thanked me for it! This gift had made a way, and this had challenged my thinking!

FOCUS FOR CONFESSION

Father, I thank you for the accuracy of your word. I thank you that I can trust your word to always find the mark and to be able to reveal the sin that needs to be exposed. As I soak in your word, I know your word can liberate me completely. I trust you to teach me how to think in the opposite spirit to the culture around me. Teach me to be generous in blessing others. Amen.

DAY 28

When I came to you, brothers, I did not come with eloquence or superior wisdom as I proclaimed to you the testimony about God... so that your faith might not rest on men's wisdom, but on God's power. We do, however, speak a message of wisdom among the mature, but not the wisdom of this age or of the rulers of this age, who are coming to nothing. No, we speak of God's secret wisdom, a wisdom that has been hidden and that God destined for our glory before time began.

1 CORINTHIANS 2:1, 5–7

THOUGHT FOR REFLECTION

Remember, we are never asked to serve God because of our ability, but because of our destiny. God is always able to fill the gap and make us what we need to be to get the job done. We need to realize that the testimony of what God has done will always be more convincing than our ability to argue clever points of theology. When you can look someone in the eyes and say, "I know that I know this is true because I have experienced it", people's arguments evaporate. So when we share about God, our success does not rely on our intellectual prowess or our sophisticated debating skills but on the raw evidence of our experience. We need to come and confidently proclaim our story about God in our life. The simple stories of God's goodness are as powerful as the account of a miraculous healing. But we need to let the revelatory power of God's wisdom direct our topics of conversation. We must let our knowledge combine with God's power, and discover true wisdom. This will be an incredible combination!

Travelling on the train to London God gave me a word of wisdom. As I entered the carriage, there was a woman sitting opposite me and she looked stressed and anxious. I asked her if she was worried about her day and she immediately looked nervous and was hesitant to talk. So I prayed and asked for wisdom: should I keep talking and, if so, what should I say? I felt to ask her another question, and so enquired if I could pray for her as I felt she was burdened with fear and God wanted to help her. Her eyes welled up with tears and then she spoke to me. On the way to the train, she told me she had asked God that if He cared for her, and was alive, please would He send her a message of hope. She was attending the final day of a court case that involved her marriage and her business, and was terrified that she would lose everything she loved and owned. Then she turned to me and asked – "Do you have a message from God for me?" I was shocked that suddenly she was asking such a direct question, and felt I had no real answers for her. So I prayed again – "God, please give me wisdom!" Immediately, I remembered I had the "Message Bible" in my bag, and gave it to her saying here was a message from God for her. She immediately opened the Bible and read the first passage she found, and began to cry! She had opened the Bible to Matthew chapter 6, verse 27, "Who of you by worrying can add a single hour to his life?" She continued reading, and I watched the wisdom of God do its work in her life!

FOCUS FOR CONFESSION

Father, I thank you that you are not limited by my knowledge, but that you increase my understanding with your divine wisdom. Show me the power of my testimony working together with your power in lives around me. Please let me overcome every sense of inferiority concerning my intellectual capacity. Teach me to access your secret wisdom for my life. Thank you for activating my thinking with your power. Amen.

WEEK 5

ANCHORED IN HIS LOVE

DAY 29

He has taken me to the banquet hall, and his banner over me is love. Strengthen me with raisins, refresh me with apples.

SONG OF SOLOMON 2:4–5

We are being positioned in a new place, seated in the banqueting hall of heaven! Often, we can feel that we are just clawing our way through life, only just surviving without any joy. But we must remember that we are made to thrive, not just survive. Even in the wilderness seasons of life, we can flourish and turn these desert times into seasons of strength and growth. We are destined to complete the race looking like a champion; we will more than just make it around the track of life, and we can finish this race with excellence. How can we know this? We will do this because we are resourced by the power of the love of God. Those tough seasons will deepen our roots into the goodness of God and produce a harvest of godly character. God loves you, and as this truth penetrates your thinking, you will realize that He created you to overcome in every area of your life. He has seated you with Him at the very celebration table of victory. The love of God NEVER fails! He has seated you

under this banner of the unfailing love of God, and this love speaks victory to all opposition!

When we walk through the dark seasons, we must remember our true identity and position. Let nothing take the knowledge of the love of God away from you. You are a focus of His love and adoration. We all have times when we battle with the assurance of whose we are, and what God has called us to be. In these seasons, we need to run and hide under this banner of love. Anchor your emotions in the revelation that your "daddy" in heaven HAS chosen you. Let the harvest of yesterday, the fruitfulness of your labour, the testimonies of the partnership of God, and your working together, strengthen your resolve to stand. Let each memory of the goodness of God, like grapes harvested last season, now become the raisins that feed your soul today. For we overcome the enemy by the word of our testimony. So remember what God has done for you, and through you. Eat this fruit and be strong! Let the refreshment of the harvests around you refresh you, too: look at the "apples" being reaped around you. Eat and know that your God has placed you in a fruitful place and be strengthened by the fruitfulness all around you.

So allow God to take you to His banqueting hall, and let your spirit be strengthened with a fresh revelation that you are loved. Kill every lie of rejection. Be refreshed deep within your being and know you are precious. Your life is positioned by the love of God for breakthrough and success. So live life with a smile, knowing you were created to live life utterly satisfied!

FOCUS FOR CONFESSION

Father, I trust you to seat me in a safe place where you will reveal your love for me. I trust you to protect me and cover me with a banner of victory. Father, I know you have the perfect food to strengthen my body and refresh my spirit. Let me know the sound of victory in every area of my life as I rest secure in your love. Thank you for the sound of celebration I can hear in my spirit as I sit at the banqueting table with you. Let me be rooted in a deep revelation of your love for me. Amen.

DAY 30

The Lord appeared to us in the past, saying: "I have loved you with an everlasting love; I have drawn you with loving-kindness. I will build you up again and you will be rebuilt, O Virgin Israel. Again you will take up your tambourines and go out to dance with the joyful."

JEREMIAH 31:3–4

THOUGHT FOR REFLECTION

As the tears and mascara flowed down her face, I stood and watched with wonder at the love of God. This precious girl came from a Christian home, but after her father had been discovered having an affair, she had lost her home

and her walk with God. But tonight God had stretched out His hand and touched her. She had wandered into the service with a friend after much persuasion. During the service, I had approached her and asked permission to share a word with her. Calling her by name, I told her that God had given me her name as a sign, because He wanted her to know that she was precious and He had not forgotten her face. But He also wanted to restore joy to her life again, and awaken the dancer and creativity in her life that had been so crushed. So here she lay on the floor still crying two hours later! Finally, she lifted her head, and over the next few hours told me her story; an amazing fact was that on that very day in desperation she had called out to God on the street. A short while later, a girlfriend saw her in the street and persuaded her to come to the service with her; then, through my word, God called her by name. More amazingly, the last thing she remembered doing in church, before the trouble with her Dad had blown her family and world apart, was a dance and drama evening where she had danced. Tenderly, the Lord appeared to her saying, "I love you", and suddenly the past years of isolation disappeared, and she sobbed as God touched her again.

I believe that God is a great restorer. The enemy comes to steal and crush our destiny, but God always comes to rebuild and lift us back to our right position.

But when we are wounded, we need the gentle sound of His love to give us confidence to step out once again. He captivates us with His voice, and so draws us out of our hiding place and woos us to stand tall again. As we align our lives back within the love of God, suddenly we feel secure once again, and joy bubbles up in our spirit. We find that we cannot help but worship, dance and celebrate. We know the security of being anchored in this vast love again, and we cannot help but celebrate!

FOCUS FOR CONFESSION

Father, thank you that you have appeared to me with a fresh revelation of your love again and again. Thank you that I know you will come personally to me just as you have done in the past to touch me again as I wait for you. Father, I thank you for your voice of love which draws me and builds me up. I thank you that you know exactly how to connect with me and restore me again. Father, I believe days of dancing, celebration and great joy are ahead. I will be securely anchored in your love and carry a new freedom in my life. Thank you for your tender voice of love. Amen.

DAY 31

The Lord your God is with you, he is mighty to save. He will take great delight in you, he will quiet you with his love, he will rejoice over you with singing.

ZEPHANIAH 3:17

THOUGHT FOR REFLECTION

You are not alone. God is with you, watching you, guiding your decisions and always ready to save you from harm. As we learn the sound of His voice we will recognize the sense of God warning us and so avoid many mistakes. I remember when the children were small I would often feel this sense of ill ease and realize this was God talking. One time the house was too quiet and I realized the children were upstairs. As I mounted the last stair I caught a glimpse of my son, scissors in hand, about to cut my daughter's hair. After all, they only wanted to play "hairdressers", but this would have been a disaster as Nicola was about to be a bridesmaid at a wedding in a few weeks! Remember, God is with you and He is mighty enough to save us, both from these smaller domestic disasters and the larger life crises. He is a mighty saviour. He can rescue children from drugs, husbands from violence, women from depression and you from

your poor choices. He is mighty when He saves.

The way in which God saves us is so incredible. He chases us with passionate love. It is this sound of His overwhelming love that triggers the rescue mission. It is the goodness of God that causes us to turn our lives around and make wise choices. We repent because we are challenged by love and not harsh confrontation. As you stop and listen to the sound of His deep love for you, it changes you in the core of your being. This love calms the raging storms of emotional pain and disturbing memories. His love can turn around the anxious mind and bring it to peace. You can stop running away from your fears and rest in a tranquil place. He delights in you, hushes you and then sings over you! The right song and music, at the right moment, can open your heart like nothing else. We have all watched those romantic moments in a film and been gripped by the atmosphere created by the music at the perfect moment. But here the God of all creation creates your intimate moment for you. He sings over you, dispelling all the other negative sounds. He wants you to enter the resting place where you know that you are special, cherished and loved, and whatever the circumstances, He wants you to hear His song in the depth of your being.

So take a moment right now and be secured in His love once again. Can you hear His song? Listen, wait and enjoy – it is the Father singing over you!

FOCUS FOR CONFESSION

Father, when I cannot worship I thank you that I can hear you sing. Father, when I cannot fight I thank you that you can save me. God, I thank you that I can know you, and you are mighty and able to save me. Father, I thank you that you take great delight in me and you comfort me with your love. You love me and rejoice over me; let me hear your celebration over my life. Let me see your face of love. Thank you, Father, that you watch over me. Amen.

DAY 32

I pray that out of his glorious riches he may strengthen you with power through his Spirit in your inner being, so that Christ may dwell in your hearts through faith. And I pray that you, being rooted and established in love, may have power, together with all the saints, to grasp how wide and long and high and deep is the love of Christ.

EPHESIANS 3:16–18

THOUGHT FOR REFLECTION

Praying the prayers of Scripture have real power. You can declare them with confidence knowing this prayer comes straight from the heart of heaven. This particular prayer in Ephesians, chapter three, gives us powerful access to His supernatural love for us. We all discover our "love challenges" soon enough; maybe someone joins your Bible study group and their contribution and manner just irritates you, or even worse, you are given a new challenging boss who you have to work with in close proximity every day! Suddenly, you realize you need a "love capacity" upgrade. Then this is the prayer for you. I remember when I was challenged to pray for nations and specific people, but found I had no fluency of language. I struggled to pray. Then the Holy Spirit spoke to me – "Rachel, stop **trying** to pray – first let me touch your heart and teach you to love!"

We need to realize that this love has a spiritual source and does not flow from our natural ability. We all find it difficult to love someone when there is no natural chemistry or connection. But God roots us in this love of the Holy Spirit, which is triggered by a decision of faith rather than our emotions, and we find that we can love even if we do not feel we want to love them. This love becomes a decision of your will. God's love is so high and wide and long and deep. It will always challenge you to move out beyond your comfort zones, and stretch you to love the unlovely and the unlikeable!

As God roots and anchors you in His love, your personal love capacity and ability to love others will change. You will have a new understanding of His amazing love and it will grip you with wonder. God is love, and as we move "God-ward" and touch His heart, He moves us "man-ward" with a heart of generosity. Our heart is touched with the Father's heart of love. We find we can pray and give to people we would usually ignore. We find intercession does not flow out of our personality, but it is a ministry of love. As the revelation of the passionate love of God touches our heart, we begin to feel this passion for other people and start to pray with a new fluency. Suddenly, we understand that people matter to

God and that they are His most prized possessions! It is only as we are deeply rooted in this revelation ourselves, that we find we also begin to demonstrate His love for others in prayer and action. So, today, take some time and ponder on this vast, incredible love of God for you and others. Know that you are utterly loved, and then receive this love afresh, and become a lover of people! Begin to give this love away wherever you go!

FOCUS FOR CONFESSION

Lord, let my life be strongly rooted in a new level of revelation of your love for me. I thank you so much for this greater understanding of your love in my life. Father, I want my eyes to be opened to the next season of your love for me and through me. I want a fresh touch of this love to stretch me to become a lover of you and others. Help me overcome my "love challenges" with your supernatural love. Father, establish me in this love, give me more power to know this love and let it fill me so that I overflow. I know this must be a secure anchor in my life! Amen.

DAY 33

Love is patient, love is kind. It does not envy, it does not boast, it is not proud. It is not rude, it is not self-seeking, it is not easily angered, it keeps no record of wrongs. Love does not delight in evil but rejoices with the truth. It always protects, always trusts, always hopes, always perseveres. Love never fails.

1 CORINTHIANS 13:4–8

THOUGHT FOR REFLECTION

The love of God is so expressive and creates such an atmosphere of affirmation. As you consider each of these statements describing His love, imagine what an incredible environment this true love of God builds. I remember watching Gordon teaching our daughter to ride her first two-wheel bike. He spent hours chasing her across the grass as she wobbled, fell off, cried and then refused to try again, but he patiently picked her up, wiped her tears, persuaded her to try again, and chased her once more. I remember watching the effect of Gordon's patient love on Nicola after each failed attempt as she tried to master riding her bike. She would ask him, "Please help me, I can't do it, I am no good!" Gordon would reply, "Nicola, you are the best and

I love you, and of course you can do it!" Slowly, the fear of balancing disappeared under the sound of Gordon's constant patience and affirmation, and suddenly she was off, stable and secure screaming, "Daddy I can do it, you are right!"

Take a few moments to consider the powerful statements of the dimensions of this love. Reflect on the people that God has put in your world to express this love to you, and be a good receiver. For as we become good receivers, we can then become good releasers of His love, too. If we live by this code of conduct, then people will always be soaked in the love of God whenever they are with us. God is such a great encourager; His sound in my life is always one of great strengthening. There is no competition and jostling for position, no anger or injustice, but He creates a safe place where dreams and hope can grow. God is also ready to walk the distance with us, He is not here today and gone tomorrow, but He desires to work with us until we conquer the fears. His love is patient and perseveres.

This love never fails! Like water, if we will begin to pour out this love on thirsty ground it will find a way to soak the dry soil of people's hearts. Water has an amazing knack of finding its way into every crack if it is poured out! So just let this love flow. Remember love never fails. It can soften the hardest heart, and often when it seems it is having no effect something is happening under the surface! So become a stubborn lover, and keep wetting people around you with this incredible love of God.

FOCUS FOR CONFESSION

I thank you, Father, for the expression of kind, patient love shown to me through people around me. Teach me to believe that love expressed through people can be trusted and does not always have an agenda. Father, let me open the deep places of my life and become a good receiver from you and others. Teach me the dimensions and beauty of this true godly love. Give me fresh insight into the truth that "Love never fails!" Show me how to be a stubborn lover in the difficult times, so that I can see your love in action. Thank you. Amen.

"He who has compassion on them will guide them and lead them beside springs of water. See, they will come from afar – some from the north, some from the west, some from the region of Aswan." Shout for joy, O heavens; rejoice, O earth; burst into song, O mountains! For the Lord comforts his people and will have compassion on his afflicted ones. But Zion said, "The Lord has forsaken me, the Lord has forgotten me." Can a mother forget the baby at her breast and have no compassion on the child she has borne? Though she may forget, I will not forget you!

ISAIAH 49:10–15

THOUGHT FOR REFLECTION

His love never fails to pursue us through every step of life, but there are seasons when it feels less tangible. This is when we need to actively strengthen our anchor in the love of God. When we go through the tough times, we must know that God has compassion for us, He literally suffers with us as we walk through the challenge. Even in the midst of the trial, He wants to guide, provide and sustain us. But we must keep walking through the circumstances in faith knowing that God has not deserted us, that He still showers us with His love and

has a plan of redemption. It is easy to be anchored in His love when life feels good, but we must be mature lovers that can press on through the difficult times, too.

One of the main deceptions we receive from the enemy in the tough times is the lie that God does not care. In our pain we react against God, accusing Him of deserting us and forgetting His promises. We get offended and angry, and then withdraw our affection and lose the sense of His presence. But here God pleads with us to understand that nothing will ever remove us from His thoughts. Like a mother, He will never forget your face, your expressions, and His love for you. In fact, God emphasizes that His love is even more reliable than the strong bond created by a nursing mother towards her baby. God is with you, even if you cannot feel it so strongly in your emotions.

So, today, meditate on the goodness of the love of God. Secure the tent pegs of His love for you and remember God will never abandon you! Do not fall into the trap of agreeing with the devil's plan for your life; do not let the thoughts of being forsaken and forgotten grip your thinking. Soak yourself in His incredible love and commitment to your life. Like a boat that has hit some big waves and high winds, remember you are made to sail through these tests. God has equipped you to succeed, and once you pass the test, you discover new waters, different horizons and greater satisfaction. So remember, lean into the incredible love of God, do not let it go and you will be transformed!

FOCUS FOR CONFESSION

God, you have compassion for me and you understand my capacity. You know how to lead me and you have refreshing water ready to satisfy me. In the tough seasons, I trust you to lead me and I know that I do not need to fear being overwhelmed. Father, help me resist the lie that you have forsaken me as I know you will never forget me. Thank you so much for your love for me! Thank you so much for your gentleness and compassion when I feel weak! Make me a mature lover that can press on through the tough seasons with my knowledge of your love unshaken. Help me maintain this revelation in my spirit whatever I feel in my emotions! Thank you. Amen.

WEEK 6

ADVANCE WITH NEW STRENGTH

DAY 35

Be strong and very courageous. Be careful to obey all the law my servant Moses gave you; do not turn from it to the right or to the left, that you may be successful wherever you go. Have I not commanded you? Be strong and courageous. Do not be terrified; do not be discouraged, for the Lord your God will be with you wherever you go.

JOSHUA 1:7, 9

THOUGHT FOR REFLECTION

If God meant us to have courage, why did He give us legs? For many of us our natural response to a new challenge is to run! But in order to inherit our promises we need to stand up with a new confidence and know that God will strengthen us to accomplish our calling. It is time to cultivate a new lifestyle, where we hold our promises in our hands not just in our dreams. This takes courage! Here, God challenges Joshua to walk into the next season of his destiny and tells him to step forward with courage. Recently, my daughter gave birth to her first baby. I watched her prepare her body and emotions for this time of birthing. Suddenly, the day of the contractions arrived and we knew this baby was coming. I watched a sense of purpose grip Nicola as she knew the time of waiting had ended, and now she had to find strength and courage for birthing. Before she got into the car to leave for the hospital she looked at me with determined eyes, "Mum I can do this, I know I can, I was made for this!" This is the cry that needs to awaken in our spirits, we need to press into the next season with determined courage that will bring to birth our promises.

Mark Twain made this statement many years ago, "It is curious that physical courage should be so common in the world and moral courage so rare." We need to take up this challenge! This is the time for the church to identify the areas where moral courage has been lacking, and it is essential that we receive fresh courage if we are going to take back our ground! We are living in a season when everything that can be shaken is being shaken. The legislative structure of our nations is being changed as we yield to the pressure of a sexually promiscuous society. But we need courage to stake our ground and speak out with wisdom and authority. Joshua was promised that, "I will give you every place where you set your foot." In the same way, we need to hold fast to our confidence, and believe we can make footprints of the kingdom in the land! It is time for a new generation of courageous people who believe they have been made to break through!

Of course, we immediately recognize that this type of courage is not natural. We need to take this courage from Jesus. Remember when the disciples were terrified in the boat, Jesus spoke to them and we read in Matthew, chapter fourteen, and verse twenty seven, the following – "But Jesus immediately said to them: 'Take courage! It is I. Do not be afraid.'" So, today, whatever situation you are facing, hear the sound of the voice of Jesus. He is speaking with you, He says to you: "Do not fear – TAKE courage!" Right now, receive this strength from Him and know that you can stand and not run!

FOCUS FOR CONFESSION

Father, will you enable me to be strong and courageous in this next season. I thank you that I do not have to find this strength from my own resources. I take courage from you! Let your word equip me and enable me to be strong and courageous. Father, I know that as I am obedient and just do what the Holy Spirit tells me to do, I am able to fulfil what you have purposed for me. I thank you that I do not need to feel discouraged because you are with me. Let me have such a sense of the power and the presence of God walking with me wherever I go. Thank you that I can stand in strength in these days. Amen.

DAY 36

I took you from the ends of the earth, from its farthest corners I called you. I said, "You are my servant"; I have chosen you and have not rejected you. So do not fear, for I am with you; do not be dismayed, for I am your God. I will strengthen you and help you; I will uphold you with my righteous right hand.

ISAIAH 41:9–10

THOUGHT FOR REFLECTION

God gives you the job and then graces you with the ability! He chooses you from the most unlikely place, calls you His servant, and then strengthens you for the task. What an amazing God! When you read the Bible, it is astonishing to realize who God selected to be His authors. He chooses a murderer, a man who killed another in fear and rage, to write the first five books. Then, He selects a king who committed adultery, murder and deception to write several others! God does not dwell on our past but on our purpose! He is not afraid of our weaknesses as He knows He has the strength to make us strong if we will yield our life.

In these days, God is selecting people from unlikely places, both geographically and socially, to fulfil His plans. We just need to be flexible and let Him direct our steps. I never believed that God would use me to teach and speak in the nations. At school, conversation practice in my French classes was a major trauma and I also hated being selected to read a passage in the English class. I was terrified I would embarrass myself and I had no confidence, but with God everything changes! What others reject, God then accepts, and He trains you to be His instrument.

So, today, take time to rest in the new strength that God is giving you. Meditate on all His promises and allow Him to help you. The patterns of yesterday will not control your life any longer. God has chosen you! I remember when I was the captain of the hockey squad, we would stand with our class in front of us as the captains and we were allowed to choose our team for the friendly matches. We would see the crowd of eager faces, each ready and waiting to play; it was as if they were screaming at us – "Pick me! Pick me!" Then we had the honour of choosing who would play with us. Sometimes, I would feel sorry for certain people as I knew they were never usually chosen. So I would pick them for my team and I would always be amazed at how well they played. It was almost as if the decision to choose them boosted their confidence so that they played their best game ever. This is what I picture when

I read that God has chosen us! He has selected us to play on the kingdom's team and to work with Him. I know I am not the best player but when I play alongside Him, the standard of my game improves because He is the best! Although life is not a game, let the revelation of God choosing you to partner with Him fill you with fresh gratitude. Learn to partner with God and let Him strengthen you!

FOCUS FOR CONFESSION

Father, your call on my life has drawn me from the furthest places geographically and the deepest places emotionally. You have taken hold of me, chosen me and I know that you do not reject me. I am yours. So I will trust that you are with me, even when life does not always seem to make sense. Let me know that you are with me. Thank you for your strong arm underneath me and for your love and compassion towards me. Father, uphold me now, hold me close and let me know that I am strong and complete in you. Thank you for your strength. Amen.

DAY 37

Finally, be strong in the Lord and in his mighty power.
Put on the full armour of God so that you can take your
stand against the devil's schemes. For our struggle is not
against flesh and blood, but against the rulers, against
the authorities, against the powers of this dark world and
against the spiritual forces of evil in the heavenly realms.

EPHESIANS 6:10–12

THOUGHT FOR REFLECTION

I love this book of Ephesians which, for me, is a manual for life. It opens with focusing us on the love of our Father, then teaches us about our relationships in the church, workplace, and family, and finally instructs us how to take authority in the spiritual realms. So, here in the last chapter of Ephesians, Paul gives us one of his important "finally" instructions.

I travel regularly, and as I walk out of the house to catch my flight I usually summarize the important tasks that must not be forgotten while I am away. The final task, the one that I usually repeat several times, is the one that matters most to me! So I recognize this pattern of behaviour here in Paul's directions to the Ephesian church: "Finally," he reminds them, "remember, be strong in the Lord." So we need to hear the urgency of this statement from Paul, and ensure that we find new strength in God to stand and advance into His purpose for us. We need to realize that taking new levels of authority will always necessitate that we press through new challenges of opposition. But we need to become courageous fighters who are determined to take our position in God.

The hardest perspective to keep in check during the fierce battle is who our enemy is! So often we personalize our opponent, and fight the person rather than the spiritual atmosphere they carry. We can become consumed with suspicion towards our boss, who we believe marginalizes us deliberately and then takes credit for our work, rather than recognizing the insecurity and control that works through him. We are deeply wounded by the angry retorts of our sister at a family

gathering rather than recognizing the jealous spirit. We must understand that we are in a battle to birth our destiny, and this battle does get personal! So make sure you are struggling against the right opponent. Take a stubborn stand against the enemy and all his accusations, and rebuke the devil's schemes against you.

So, today, take a moment and reflect on the battles you need to win. Ask God to identify your real opponents, then with fresh revelation take your stand and overcome your struggles with dignity!

FOCUS FOR CONFESSION

Father, I know that my strength comes from being connected to you. I receive new strength and revelation to fight my battles. Father, teach me how to put on the armour of God so that I can take my stand against every subtle scheme of the devil. Make me more aware of the enemy's plans, and help me recognize the battle areas with the spiritual forces and overcome. I thank you so much for all the spiritual wisdom that you have given me, so that I can overcome the enemy. You have made me to be more than a conqueror as I step forward in your strength. Amen.

DAY 38

"Because of the oppression of the weak and the groaning of the needy, I will now arise," says the Lord. "I will protect them from those who malign them." And the words of the Lord are flawless, like silver refined in a furnace of clay, purified seven times. O Lord, you will keep us safe and protect us from such people forever.

PSALMS 12:5–7

THOUGHT FOR REFLECTION

God is our defender! We need to fight our battles of faith, and conquer the doubts that entangle our mind, but God will fight and defend our reputation if necessary! This is not our responsibility! One of the toughest things about loving Jesus is that not everyone will like us. We have to pay the price of being misunderstood and marginalized by friends, family and even church. Especially when we are younger, at university or just starting work, it is hard to live under the oppressive atmosphere of being ridiculed and maligned for our faith. But we need to stand straight and allow God to protect us and keep us safe. Find a hiding place in His protection and let Him speak on your behalf.

I remember a young girl weeping with me after a

Sunday service. She was the first Christian in her home, and at age seventeen was having a tough time. Her father was an alcoholic and her mum was pressured with a large family, and unable to pay the bills. Now her daughter had become "religious" and this seemed to add to, rather than relieve, her mum's pressure. "Why don't they like me now, I am a much better person, but they seem to want me to go back to drinking and partying, they will not accept me," she cried! Her heart was broken as the more she tried to serve her home and talk to them about Jesus, the more hostile the environment seemed to become. Then I explained to her that her witness had brought the light of God into the home and her family did not like the feeling of being exposed. I counselled her to stop trying to defend her actions and faith, but instead to just relax and live with them.

A year later, I was back in the church and this girl came running up with her mother beside her. "It worked," she said. Her mother then explained that when she watched her daughter begin to live her faith in the home without fighting and arguing with them about Jesus, it began to convict her. Finally, she had a dream where Jesus asked her, "Why do you reject your daughter? Can't you see that she is happy?" So, she decided to come to church and found Jesus, too. I do believe that God will defend us, but we need to lean into

His protection and let Him speak on our behalf. So often these days, people have dreams or warnings and God communicates on our behalf. So relax, continue to carry His presence and let God defend you!

FOCUS FOR CONFESSION

God, I thank you that you speak out on my behalf. You arise against all who malign me and you protect me. You know everything that happens and you hear the deep cry of my heart when I encounter injustice. Thank you, Father, that you can protect my reputation. Thank you that I can trust you to speak out at the right time, Father, that I can trust that your words will be perfect in every situation. Thank you, Father, that you defend me against people who wound me with their words and actions. I am safe in you! Amen.

DAY 39

It is God who arms me with strength and makes my way perfect. He makes my feet like the feet of a deer; he enables me to stand on the heights. He trains my hands for battle; my arms can bend a bow of bronze. You give me your shield of victory; you stoop down to make me great. You broaden the path beneath me, so that my ankles do not turn over. You armed me with strength for battle; you made my adversaries bow at my feet.

2 SAMUEL 22:33–40

THOUGHT FOR REFLECTION

I remember the intense arm wrestling competitions between my two brothers at home. These were fiercely competitive moments when the "big" brother's honour was at stake. My brothers have a ten year age gap between them, so the day my baby brother could win this contest would be a landmark occasion! Often, I think of this when we are in the intense heat of a faith battle. You feel that your life depends on winning this match, and you know your arm needs to find every ounce of strength to hold out and not lose its grip. So when you feel you cannot hold on any longer, let God come and arm you with strength. Maybe your hope for your children's salvation is wavering, let God quicken your arm of faith today. Usually, the reason why one of my brothers relinquished their grip was that they got cramp in their muscles and they had to let go. I learned that it was the strength of the perseverance of their grip that won these arm wrestling matches, not the power of their muscles! I believe it is the same for us, we need to learn how to hold our position of faith and not let go!

God can prepare you to be a champion. Today, take some time to consider your circumstances with Him: go and stand on the heights with Him. So often when we are in the battle we get locked into one perspective and we lose our vision. We need God to take us up onto the heights and to show us what He sees. Let God strengthen your arm of battle, but grace your feet with a lightness

of step in His presence. Let a new spring come into your step and enjoy the BIG picture with God.

Begin to let God show you what victory looks like, let Him show you the broad path, let Him show you what the enemy really looks like when you have your armour in place, and the arrows of His word in your hand. Dream with God on the mountain heights of intimacy, get refreshed and then win the battles of life like a champion!

FOCUS FOR CONFESSION

So strengthen me, God, and make my way perfect. Help me walk like the deer with nimble feet that are quick on the mountains. Let me find my place on the mountain tops with you again. Give me a spirit of warfare and train my hands to battle on behalf of the broken and hurting. Let me find my language of worship and warfare. Thank you that I walk out of this season rebuilt, with a new inner peace and carrying a shield of victory. I can walk with dignity, knowing that I will not stumble and my ankles will not turn. You give me strength so that I can endure in the battle until the time of breakthrough is mine. Amen.

DAY 40

You will go out in joy and be led forth in peace; the mountains and hills will burst into song before you, and all the trees of the field will clap their hands. Instead of the thornbush will grow the pine tree, and instead of briers the myrtle will grow. This will be for the Lord's renown, for an everlasting sign, which will not be destroyed.

ISAIAH 55:12–13

THOUGHT FOR REFLECTION

You have walked this "Pathway of Peace" for forty days and you need to know that you have started on a path that can last forever. For you will go out with joy and be led forth in peace continually. God has done a new work of imparting new confidence and strength into your life. You have altered your lifestyle and learnt to rest and absorb His peace rather than carry your cares. You have trained your ear to recognize the sound of your Father's voice and practised cultivating a deeper level of security in your life. You have taught yourself to ignore the distractions that quickly divert your attention from your godly calling. You understand the battleground of your mind and know how to win the war more frequently. So it is time to go forth into a new season anchored in His love and equipped with new strength. You are ready to step out with joy and be led forth with peace.

Let the Holy Spirit open your eyes anew to see the world around you, celebrating your freedom. Creation loves to watch the children of God step into their destiny, free from their pain. Expect to see breakthrough in your relationships with people at work. Where you have known the betrayal and wounding of the thornbush in the past, now you will watch the strong pine trees of protection grow. Where your life has been caught in the briers of worry and anxiety, now you will know the sweet fragrance of the myrtle in your life. This is a day of transition, where you walk out with joy knowing a sense of freedom and peace.

So receive His peace and walk free! The work that God has done in your life over these last weeks is not just a quick fix that will disappear. No, God promises you today that this work will last forever. So ask God to give you a confirming sign today of His work in your life. Look out for a God signature that confirms His commitment to you. God will communicate with you, so walk out with expectation that God will give you a sign that this is the beginning of the rest of your life!

I remember praying for a young man who was so filled with anxiety, but needed to apply for a new job. He was terrified of making the wrong move and could not

hear God. So we prayed together, and I encouraged him to look for a sign from God to help him know that God was leading him. He finally applied for a new job in London, and was then called for interview, and phoned us to pray as he was still concerned he may make the wrong choice. So Gordon and I reminded him to look for his God signature. A few hours later he phoned excited and confident. He had got his job and was overjoyed! "Why are you so convinced it is the right move?" we asked him. "Oh", he replied, "I forgot to mention that on my way to the company, as I stepped out of the underground train station, a man was pasting a new billboard sign on the wall. The advert was huge and read – "Time for Change, Time to move!" So get ready for a God encounter, and live the rest of your life on this "Pathway of Peace"!

Focus for Confession

So, as I enter a new season in my life, I know there is one constant: YOU are with me! Nothing can separate me from your love. I have been through some tough times, but I have discovered no one satisfies me like you, Jesus. Today I know I can overcome all fear and walk out with a new tranquillity and peace. Your love has pursued me, your love has strengthened me and your love has rescued me and made me secure. Thank you for your courage that makes me more than a conqueror. You have armed me for battle and secured me in your strength. I will stand firm, knowing I am loved, and rest secure with my mind at peace. Thank you for this miracle. Amen!

Rachel Hickson is an internationally respected prayer leader and Bible teacher with a recognized prophetic gift. She teaches all over the world, and is in demand as a conference speaker. At the age of twenty-four, Rachel, with her husband, Gordon, worked alongside Reinhard Bonnke and the Christ for All Nations team in Africa. After just six weeks in Zimbabwe, she almost lost her life in an horrific car accident, but was miraculously healed by God. This incident brought to birth in Rachel a desire to pray and to train other people, to realize the full potential of a praying church.

After returning from Africa in 1990, Rachel and her husband, Gordon, pastored a group of four churches in Hertfordshire and it was during this time that they established "Heartcry Ministries", with the call to train and equip people to be released into effective prayer and intercession for their communities, cities and nations. In

2005, Rachel and Gordon moved to be based in Oxford, where Gordon is associate minister on the staff of St Aldate's Church.

Rachel travels internationally, visiting Europe, North America, Africa and India. Invitations come from various denominational backgrounds, where a passion for unity has brought the churches together to pray for a move of God in their area. Rachel and Gordon have a passion to see cities transformed through the power of prayer and evangelism. One of their projects links churches and prayer ministries across London, which has developed a city strategy called the "London Prayernet" (www.londonprayer.net).

Rachel has been married to Gordon for over twenty-eight years. She is a mother of two grown-up children, Nicola and David, and she has one grandchild, Leila.

She is the author of four books: *Supernatural Communication: The Privilege of Prayer*, and *Supernatural Breakthrough: The Heartcry for Change*, published by New Wine Ministries; and *Stepping Stones to Freedom*, and *Eat the Word, Speak the Word*, published by Monarch.

We work with churches and people from many nations and denominations to equip them in the following areas:

- PRAYER – Training an army of ordinary people in Prayer Schools and seminars to become confident to break the sound barrier and pray informed, intelligent and passionate prayers.

- PROPHETIC – Equipping the church to be an accurate prophetic voice in the nation by teaching in training schools and conferences the principles of the prophetic gift. We seek to train people who are passionate to know the presence of God, are available to hear His voice and then learn to speak His word with accuracy so that lives can be touched and changed.

- WOMEN – Delivering a message of hope to women across the nations and cultures to help them arise with a new confidence, so that they can be equipped and ready to fulfil their destiny and execute their kingdom purpose.

- CAPITAL CITIES – Standing in the capital cities of the world, working with government institutions, businesses and the church and then crying out for a new alignment of the natural and spiritual government in these places.

A cry for London and beyond. (www.londonprayer.net).

- BUSINESS & FINANCE – Connecting business people with their kingdom purpose, so that provision can partner more effectively with vision and accelerate the purpose of God in nations. Connecting commerce, community, and church for change!

- LEADERS OF TOMORROW – Mentoring and encouraging younger leaders to pioneer the next move of God in the areas of politics and government, social action and justice issues, creative arts, media, and the ministry.

- NATIONS – Partnering with nations in Africa, the Middle East and India by supplying teaching, training and practical resources to strengthen and resource them as they work for breakthrough in their nations.

- MEDIA, TV & SATELLITE – Developing training materials to equip and disciple the church in the nations to understand and fulfil their responsibility. Being a voice of encouragement through TV into the homes of the army of ordinary people praying for impossible situations.

- RESOURCES & CONFERENCES – Writing books, manuals and training materials that will equip the church to be prepared. Running conferences and training days where leaders and the church can be encouraged to continue in their purpose and calling.

Heartcry hopes to continue strengthening the church to connect with their community, while encouraging the people to hear the urgent call to prayer. Now is the time to pray and cry out for our land and continent and watch what God will do for us!

Heartcry Ministries
P.O. Box 737
Oxford, Oxon
OX1 9FA   UK

www.heartcry.co.uk , www.heartcry.us
www.londonprayer.net